FUN IN
THE
BAHAMAS

FODOR'S

FUN IN THE BAHAMAS

1988

Anita Gates

Published by
FODOR'S TRAVEL PUBLICATIONS, INC.
New York & London

917.296

ISBN 0–679–01505–1
ISBN 0–340–41960–1 (Hodder & Stoughton)

New titles in the series

Barbados

Jamaica

also available

Acapulco

Disney World and the Orlando Area

Las Vegas

London

Maui

Montreal

New Orleans

New York City

Paris

Rio

St. Martin/Sint Maarten

San Francisco

Waikiki

MANUFACTURED IN THE UNITED STATES OF AMERICA
10 9 8 7 6 5 4 3 2 1

Contents

Maps and Plans

FUN IN THE BAHAMAS

An Overview

In Paradise Island, the casinos glitter and buzz with perfumed vacationers, clattering roulette balls, and coins tumbling from the quarter slots. In Little Exuma, the only sound is the tide splashing onto a white-sand shore.

On Nassau's Cable Beach, poolside sunbathers can enjoy a swimming contest, fashion show, and steel band concert in a single afternoon. At the Abaco Inn's cliffside pool, the ocean view is the only entertainment guests want or need.

The ads all say, "It's better in the Bahamas." Perhaps that's so, but what's better? And exactly where in the Bahamas? One island can be as different from another as the beaches at Malibu are from those on Martha's Vineyard.

Whether you're looking for the best scuba diving in the world, the most beautiful secluded beaches, the finest boating, the most dazzling casinos, the wildest shopping spree, or the liveliest limbo, you *can* find it in the Bahamas. Just not necessarily all in the same place.

The water is definitely better in the Bahamas. Throughout the islands it is incredibly clear and often incredibly calm, which makes diving, snorkeling, and

I

swimming better in the Bahamas. It's little wonder so many of those travel ads include a scene of sand and sea.

The name "Bahamas" is Spanish for shallow water (*bajamar*), but it sounds a more romantic note. The Bahamas' almost 700 islands and cays stretch more than 700 miles—from Grand Bahama Island (off the southeast coast of Florida) to Inagua (off Cuba's eastern coast). And although only 20 or so are inhabited, there are at least that many kinds of vacation possibilities among them.

Each island has its own character, but a few things are universally Bahamian. One is conch (pronounced *konk*), that ubiquitous seafood found on every menu from Nassau to Stella Maris. You may become quite fond of conch fritters, the chewy little fried hors d'oeuvres that many hotels serve up at happy hour, or of conch chowder, or of any of this delicacy's many incarnations served as a main course.

Another universal is rum drinks. Dubbed with catchy names, they're served to short-sighted tourists who've forgotten (since the last vacation) exactly what a combination hangover/sunburn feels like. Some of the most popular concoctions are the Bahama Mama, Yellow Bird, and Goombay Smash (originally a P.R. stunt to promote the off-season Goombay festival and now better known than the event).

The third thing you'll find throughout the Bahamas is Androsia, the beautiful batik resortwear made on the island of Andros. You'll see it in almost every hotel shop and shopping center, at fashion shows around every pool, and on a number of your fellow tourists.

PROVIDENCE AND PARADISE

Nassau is the Bahamas' capital city and the first stop for most visitors. Set on New Providence Island, it is also the Commonwealth's most versatile vacation spot. There's a tour or scheduled event for every taste and a variety of restaurants that range from barefoot casual to candle-light elegant.

You're most likely to stay in one of the large modern hotels, either in Nassau's Cable Beach area or on Paradise Island, just across the bridge. Either way, you can swim in a pool or the ocean, go snorkeling near your hotel or further away by boat trip, scuba, windsurf, and sail. And, at times, the number of people parasailing above a single beach can look like a division of paratroopers descending to liberate the Allies.

When it's cloudy, spend the day downtown on Bay Street, looking for bargain perfumes, watches, emeralds, leather goods, or just about anything else. Or get a cupful of quarters and settle in at the nearest casino.

Freeport/Lucaya on Grand Bahama Island is a gambler's paradise, with two casinos and an international shopping center where visitors can spend their winnings on goods from around the world. Lucaya, on the beach, is the more casual side of town, and a mecca for divers.

OUT IN THE FAMILY ISLANDS

And then there are the Out Islands. A few years ago, the government decreed that they should be referred to as the Family Islands, ostensibly to help the people who live there feel more a part of the Commonwealth. Others say it was to take their minds off the deplorable roads and the even worse phone service.

No matter what the government's motives, the name has all the wrong connotations for prospective vacationers. A Family Island sounds like a place with swing sets—perfect for the kids. The term Out Islands describes them best: remote, cut off (beautifully!) from urban life, and blessedly underdeveloped.

One piece of advice: When you decide to vacation in the Out Islands, quickly adopt an old-money attitude toward what constitutes a fine resort. Even in the best hotels here, conditions may border on the rustic. TV is rare, telephones in the guest rooms rarer, air-condition-

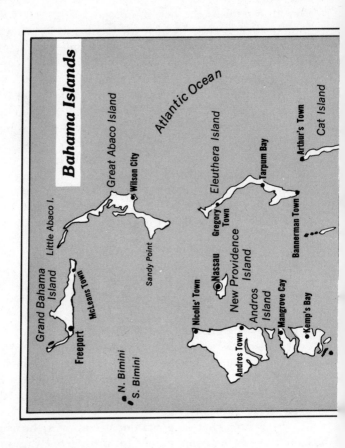

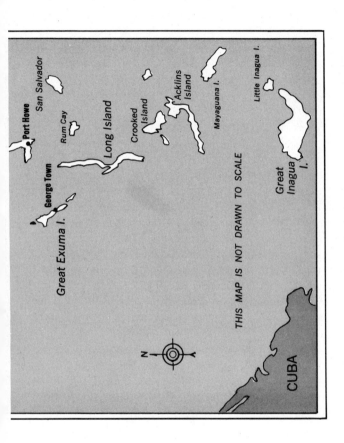

ing basically unnecessary, and decor unimpressive. But the food can be fabulous, the casual mood contagious, and the Bahamian waters incomparable. There is no better vacation spot for mellowing out fast.

Eleuthera is perhaps the best known of the Out Islands, with each of its towns a destination unto itself. Harbour Island, to the north, attracts a combination of old money and young boaters and divers to its pink-sand resorts. Governor's Harbour, farther south, is dominated by a Club Med devoted primarily to scuba diving. Still farther south, there are elegant resorts and homes in Winding Rock, Windermere, and Rock Sound.

Abaco is the next most developed Out Island, but don't let that frighten you. This is a boater's paradise, friendly to a fault. Treasure Cay is the most formal, as is the resort of the same name. Green Turtle Cay has two resorts popular with yachtsmen, honeymooners, and the world-weary of all categories. Marsh Harbour, 20 miles away, feels livelier. Boaters and U.S. vacationers keep the mood casual, but there's some real nightlife here. To find the most secluded hotels of all, take a ferry to Hopetown.

Andros is the largest of all the islands, yet one of the least developed. Still one resort, Small Hope Bay Lodge in Andros Town, has put it on the vacationer's map. This is a paradise for divers, just off the world's third largest barrier reef.

Exuma is considered the world's best yachting destination, not only during its annual Regatta but year-round for the Americans who love the challenge of its cays. George Town is the center of activity, with several small hotels and an almost rowdy nightlife of locals and visiting boaters. Some of the Bahamas' most beautiful beaches are here, too, particularly on Little Exuma and on Stocking Island. Bonefishing is another big attraction here.

Bimini is Hemingway country, the big-game fishing capital of the world, and exists almost exclusively for these purposes. The mood is American, with rock music constantly in the background and Florida sportsmen dominating the guest registers.

And then there are the other Out Islands—some with only one resort or a few tiny guest houses, but all with some special appeal. The "Far Out Islands" can be wonderful places to escape completely from everyday realities.

THE BAHAMIANS

Wherever you go, you're more likely than ever to have born-and-bred Bahamians as your hosts. Independent since 1973, the Commonwealth of the Bahamas still has a British accent, but it is growing fainter every year. The charming London-born hotel manager you met on your last visit may have been booted from the job in favor of a local, thanks to the government's Bahamianization policy.

About 85 percent of all Bahamians are black, and the government is predominantly black for the first time in the islands' history. Although there seems to be little real racial conflict here, there is some resentment among Bahamians in service jobs (taxi drivers, bellmen, waiters, etc.) toward visiting Americans. This may have more to do with economic dependence on tourism than with the fact that most visitors have white skin.

If there are cultural differences between North Americans and Bahamians, they are subtle—many visitors have regretted asking their taxi drivers why the meter hadn't been turned on. Some natives can be extremely sensitive to doubts about their honesty (particularly when warranted) and have quick tempers when accused. A number of Bahamians appear to consider it a loss of face not to know the answer to every question they're asked. So when you ask how much a taxi will cost from Point X to Point Y, you may get a very self-assured answer that has no relation to reality. On the other hand, you may get a friendly, honest, accurate, and charming reply and even make a new friend.

Religion is an important part of many Bahamians' lives. In Harbour Island, for instance, many souvenir stands bear the message, "God bless you." And even in Nassau, you may go up to the poolside snack bar and find the employees engaged in a heated philosophical discussion of the Ten Commandments.

Women will be glad to hear that the verbal-abuse quotient is quite low here. On the streets of Nassau, in fact, Bahamian men tend to whistle at and make remarks only to the local women. If a resident makes comments about a tourist wearing a swimsuit on the street, he's more likely to be expressing disapproval of her fashion *faux pas* than interest in her favors.

So just unpack your bags, put away anything fussy or uncomfortable for the next few days or weeks, amble down to the beach, sink into the warm, clear Atlantic, and get your hair wet.

That's better.

General Information

With an average winter temperature of 70 degrees and an average summer day at 81 degrees, the Bahamas are a year-round destination. Yet there are definite high and low seasons.

If you are taking a winter vacation, remember that the Bahamas are not technically in the Caribbean. Most of the best-known islands are just east of Florida, and the southernmost destinations are still well north of Haiti and Puerto Rico. Although winter temperatures rarely fall below 60, the unusual does happen. And a few resorts take pride in telling you that they've actually used their big, normally decorative fireplaces during Christmas and January chills.

Summer is the rainy season, and the islands get an average of 46 inches per year. Happily, Bahamian rain-storms are usually gentle and brief. Many seasoned travelers don't even bother to get out of the pool, knowing the storm will be over before they could towel themselves dry.

High season is winter, of course—usually early December through Easter or mid-April, whichever comes later. And although daytime weather may be much the same here in January or July, your fellow visitors are likely to be very different from season to season.

Those who winter in the Bahamas tend to be older, richer, and from more distant places; there are more northeasterners, for instance. Those who come in the summer tend to be younger, more budget-minded and more often from Florida or other parts of the South. "In the winter, most of the travelers checks we get at the front desk are fifties and hundreds," reports one hotelier. "In the summer, they're tens and twenties." Honeymooners come at all times of year.

To every rule, there is an exception—and some islands experience a completely different cycle. At the dive resorts, like Small Hope Bay Lodge on Andros, June is just as busy as February. And at Bimini, where the number of visitors is governed by the kind of fish that are biting, summer is by far the busiest time of the year.

Most Bahamian resorts stay open year-round; of those that close temporarily, most take a one- or two-month break between August and October.

WHAT TO WEAR

Your wardrobe depends on your destination and on how you plan to spend your days and nights.

Nassau is the big city of the Bahamas and demands a little more formality than other locations. Most Nassau and Paradise Island hotels are accustomed to guests walking in or near the lobby in swimsuits, preferably with cover-ups. If there's a separate pool elevator, use it. If not, make it clear that you're just passing through.

A shopping expedition to Bay Street or to Freeport's International Bazaar calls for real clothes, not beachwear. Modest shorts, jeans, or cotton pants, worn with any not-too-bare top, is fine shopping wear for men or women. Sundresses with comfortable sandals also can be good for this. (Even in the very casual Out Islands, local residents frown on swimsuits on the streets. Worse yet, they make comments about them as the guests pass.)

There's not a single restaurant in the Bahamas at which you wouldn't feel comfortable dressed very casually for lunch. Dinner is another matter. At the more elegant restaurants, jackets are required for men. Ties are still optional. However, many business travelers come to Nassau and Paradise Island, and they tend to wear ties—so gentlemen may want to go along with the trend. For women, dressing up for an elegant dinner means putting on any nice sundress or pants outfit, but with dressy sandals. Female business travelers and Bahamian women in business probably will wear panty hose, but you don't have to. After all, this *is* a vacation.

The only visitors who get really dressed up are those at conventions, with their business images in mind. You'll see them at the Cable Beach or the Paradise Towers and other hotels that cater to these groups.

The Out Islands dress code, by comparison, makes Nassau casual look like opening night at the opera. The rule: Never dress up for anything. Even the hotel managers often wear T-shirts and shorts on the job.

On most Out Islands, you'll be able to have breakfast and lunch in the sloppiest of resort wear. T-shirts and shorts, swimsuits and cover-ups, bare feet or flip-flops are fine. So is wet hair.

People on the Out Islands do tend to change clothes for dinner. That is, they shower, shampoo their hair, and put on a different set of casual clothes. Men can get away with shorts at many Out Island resorts. So can women, but most prefer to wear sundresses—either with bare feet or flat sandals.

One notable exception to this rule is Treasure Cay in Abaco. Although quite casual during the day, its restaurants call for men in jackets at dinnertime.

One other wardrobe note: If you're going to the Bahamas in winter, do pack a light jacket or sweater. Chances are you won't need it, but the evenings do occasionally turn chilly.

WHAT TO PACK

If you have a favorite suntan lotion, pick up an extra tube at home and toss it into your bag. One Nassau company dominates the Bahamas sun-care market with its own brands, although Coppertone and Sea & Ski turn up regularly. Bain de Soleil and other brands, however, are hard to find.

If you're planning to stay in a cottage, villa, or any kind of resort in which you'll have to walk back to your room on dark pathways, bring a flashlight. Some resorts light the grounds adequately; others may not. The flashlight could come in handy, too, if you get lost (or change your mind) during a romantic moonlit stroll.

And if you're visiting the Out Islands, take insect repellent. Brands like Cutter's really work, and the comfort can make a big difference as you attempt to relax by the sea.

TIME

The Bahamas are on Eastern time. If it's 12 noon in the Bahamas, it's 9 A.M. in California, 10 A.M. in Phoenix, 11 A.M. in Chicago, and 12 noon in New York.

SEASONAL EVENTS

Most of the Bahamas' big annual events require reservations months (or more) in advance. The Family Island Regatta in Exuma, Abaco's fishing tournament (both in April), and Bimini's blue marlin tournament (in June) are examples. The year's most colorful Junkanoo parades are held on Boxing Day (December 26) and New Year's

Day throughout the islands—but that, too, means making reservations well in advance.

One of the most successful events has been the Goombay Festival each summer. Designed simply to add a little excitement to the slow off-season, Goombay has grown to include organized events almost every night, particularly in Nassau, Paradise Island, and Freeport. This can mean an outdoor festival, parade, tea party, jogging contest, or almost anything else that's fun.

Watch out for holidays that the Bahamians celebrate that are unfamiliar to us, especially if you're planning a short trip. Otherwise, you might arrive to find shops and many restaurants closed on the one day you'd planned to explore them. Whit Monday (seven weeks after Easter), Emancipation Day (first Monday in August), and Discovery Day (October 12, when else?) are among the most important.

GETTING THERE

Scheduled Airlines. Many North American visitors to the Bahamas fly to Nassau. Regularly scheduled commercial flights leave from two dozen U.S. and Canadian cities.

- Aero Coach flies from Fort Lauderdale, Jacksonville, and West Palm Beach to George Town (Exuma), Marsh Harbour (Abaco), North Eleuthera, and Treasure Cay (Abaco).
- Air Canada flies from Montreal and Toronto.
- Bahamasair, the national carrier, flies from Atlanta, Fort Lauderdale, Miami, Newark, Orlando, and Tampa.
- Bahamas Express flies from Newark to Nassau, Freeport, and Treasure Cay.
- Caribbean Express flies from Miami to George Town, North Eleuthera, Rock Sound (Eleuthera), and Freeport.
- Chalk's flies its seaplanes from Miami, Fort Lauder-

dale, and West Palm Beach to Paradise Island, Bimini,
Cat Cay, and Walker's Cay (Abaco).

- Delta Airlines flies from Atlanta, Boston, Chicago,
  Dallas, Detroit, Fort Lauderdale, and New York (JFK).
- Eastern Airlines flies from Atlanta, Boston, Chicago,
  Detroit, Fort Lauderdale, Houston, Los Angeles,
  Miami, New York, and Philadelphia.
- Gull Air flies from Miami, Orlando, West Palm Beach,
  and Fort Lauderdale to Freeport and Treasure Cay.
- Pan American World Airways flies from New York
  (JFK).
- United Airlines flies from Chicago.
- Walker's Cay Airlines flies from Fort Lauderdale to
  Walker's Cay

Charter flights are another popular way to get to the
Bahamas, particularly if you're flying directly to one of
the Out Islands. Many vacation packages include charter
flights. To make your own arrangements, contact private charter companies in major south Florida cities.
Bahamasair handles inter-island flights, most originating
in Nassau. Unfortunately, many islands can be reached
only two or three times per week.

Cruises. Half of all visitors to the Bahamas now arrive on cruise ships. The vessels that visit most often
include the following:

- *Atlantic,* Home Lines, from Fort Lauderdale (twice
  weekly).
- *Britanis,* Chandris Fantasy Cruises, from Miami (weekly).
- *Carnivale,* Carnival Cruise Lines, from Miami (twice
  weekly).
- *Dolphin IV,* Dolphin Cruises, from Miami (twice weekly).
- *Emerald Seas,* Admiral Cruise Lines, from Miami (twice
  weekly).
- *Fairsky,* Sitmar Cruises, from Fort Lauderdale (weekly).
- *Fairwind,* Sitmar Cruises, from Fort Lauderdale (weekly).

- *Galileo,* Chandris Fantasy Cruises, from Miami (weekly).
- *Homeric,* Home Lines, from Fort Lauderdale (weekly).
- *Jubilee,* Carnival Cruise Lines, from Miami (weekly).
- *Mardi Gras,* Carnival Cruise Lines, from Fort Lauderdale (twice weekly).
- *Rotterdam,* Holland America Line—Westours, from Fort Lauderdale (weekly).
- *Sagafjord,* Cunard/NAC, from Fort Lauderdale (weekly).
- *Skyward,* Norwegian Caribbean Lines, from Miami (weekly).
- *Southward,* Norwegian Caribbean Lines, from Miami (weekly).
- *Starship Oceanic,* Premier Cruise Lines, from Port Canaveral (weekly).
- *Starship Royale,* Premier Cruise Lines, from Port Canaveral (weekly).
- *Starward,* Norwegian Caribbean Lines, from Miami (weekly).
- *Sunward II,* Norwegian Caribbean Lines, from Miami (twice weekly).
- *Vistafjord,* Cunard/NAC, from Fort Lauderdale (weekly).

ENTRY

No passport is required to visit the Bahamas, as long as you're a U.S., Canadian, or British citizen planning to stay no longer than three weeks. You need proof of citizenship, however, and a birth certificate is preferred.

Hold onto the white immigration card that you're given right before you arrive in the Bahamas. When departure time comes, you won't be able to leave the country without it.

DEPARTURE

You'll pay a $5 departure tax (in either currency) when you check in for your flight home. U.S. customs is often handled in Nassau before you get on your flight, so be prepared by listing your purchases and their prices on the white card. Every U.S. citizen is allowed to bring back up to $400 worth of purchases from the Bahamas duty-free.

MONEY

There's no need to exchange money, or to visit a Bahamian bank at all. The Bahamian dollar and U.S. dollar are almost exactly equal at press time. You may pay with either currency, and your change may come back in either—or in a combination of the two. If you still have Bahamian money at departure time, exchange it at the Nassau airport's Royal Bank of Canada branch.

Most hotels, restaurants, and stores accept major credit cards, particularly American Express, MasterCard, and Visa; Diners Club and Carte Blanche are widely accepted too. You can cash traveler's checks at your hotel's front desk.

Nassau and Paradise Island

If you arrive in Nassau by cruise ship, you'll be deposited right by Rawson Square. That puts you in front of the government buildings and the statue of Queen Victoria, in the center of town and Bay Street shopping.

If you arrive by plane, however, the Nassau airport will be your first glimpse of the Bahamas. It's a long but sunny walk from the plane to the terminal, but immigration and luggage pick-up go quickly. You may be in your hotel room 45 minutes after landing.

The airport itself is surprisingly small and unappealing, when you consider that Nassau receives 700,000 foreign visitors by air every year. Whether you're coming, going, or laying over here, don't expect luxury or a great variety of activities. You'll find a small post office, a resortwear boutique (probably good for a T-shirt or two), a central counter selling perfume, a newsstand that also sells toiletries, a tourist information desk, a bank branch, a liquor store (the best-stocked outlet here), and a coffee shop (all the way down by the Bahamasair

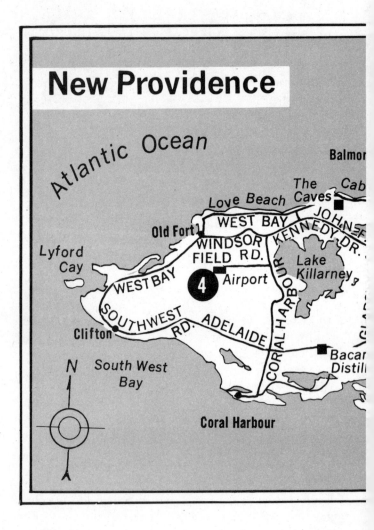

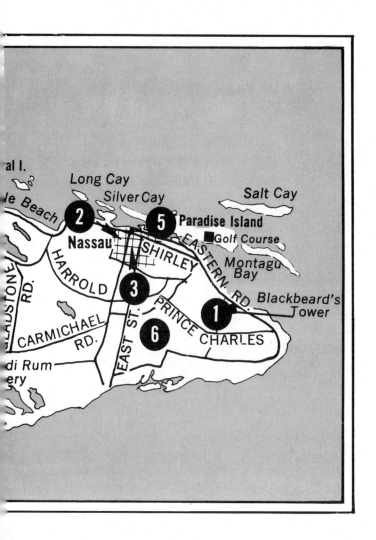

Points of Interest

1) Blackbeard's Tower
2) Fort Charlotte
3) Fort Fincastle
4) Nassau International Airport
5) Paradise Island
6) St. Augustine Monastery

domestic counters) that's primarily a stand-up or take-out affair. There is an airport restaurant, located upstairs at the northern end of the terminal, but it's recommended primarily for the desperate.

If you're leaving or arriving on a weekend, don't expect to find full services here. The bank and post office are open Monday through Friday, during normal business hours only.

If you're part of a tour group, your transportation to the hotel probably will be arranged, via mini-bus. Otherwise, you'll have to take a taxi, which you'll find just outside the terminal.

All Nassau cabs are required to have meters in good working order, but no watchdog rides along to be sure they're used. No problem; just be sure to settle on a rate *before* the cab pulls away.

You may prefer to rent a car. If you plan to do a lot of moving around during your stay, it's a good idea to contact Avis, National, or one of the local rental firms. You'll find car rental counters, both at the airport and at some hotels. At press time, rates start at about $55 per day and $300 per week, both with unlimited mileage. It may not turn out to be a lot cheaper than cabbing, but at least you'll know ahead of time what you're spending.

Nassau's hotel district is on Cable Beach, between the airport and the city. The name refers to the telegraph cable laid there in 1892 from Jupiter, Florida, to the Bahamas, but the area has a somewhat more glamorous history. As early as 1809, and throughout the 19th and early 20th centuries, horse racing was the leisure-time attraction in this part of town. Pineapple plantations took over the area later. Then the first luxury beach resorts began to be built after World War II.

Although a number of those older hotels still stand, along with apartment hotels, condominiums, and guest houses, most visitors find themselves in one of the four largest and most modern Cable Beach hotels.

The **Cable Beach Hotel,** open only since 1983, is by far the glitziest. Red brick terraces, dotted with dramatic fountains, lead to the entry. The lobby, with its plush dark green furniture, seems palatial, with modern staircases leading up to a bar and down to a restaurant.

The hallway to your right leads to the casino and conference center, but not without your passing an arcade of modern shops on both sides. They include a branch of Androsia for resortwear, the Chez Mizpah boutique for same, two jewelry stores, a liquor store, leather goods shop, large beauty salon, florist, photo shop, and drugstore. One nice thing about being in the casino hotel is that everything is open late; most shops don't close till 10 or 11 P.M.

Convention business is strong throughout the year at the Cable Beach, so the lobby is often dominated by mountains of suitcases, signaling group arrivals and departures. There also appear to be plenty of unattached guests around, both male and female. And nowhere is that more obvious than at the pool/beach area, where you might see a man in a three-piece business suit, standing in the sand to chat with a bikini-clad woman stretched out on a chaise.

You can take a private elevator to this area—it feels like a resort in itself. There are man-made rock grottos with waterfalls (including at least one that you can stand under), lots of footbridges, plus little wooden walkways and landscaped greenery near the large pool, where an amplified steel band is almost always playing.

The beach is clean and white, but narrow, with a small area roped off for swimmers. There are separate oceanside bars for food, drink, and water sports. A large patio has frosted glass tables, aqua beach chairs, off-white umbrellas, and even thatched-roof gazebos, for those who want to eat, drink, and ocean-gaze in comfortable shade. The poolside bathrooms have showers, a great convenience for sand- and salt-caked swimmers.

The rooms ($155 double and up) are among the island's most elegant, about 19 by 13 feet with plush carpet, two double beds with high bamboo headboards, chintz draperies, and a small balcony. Bathrooms have marble vanities, separate dressing areas, closets with mirrored sliding doors, complimentary shampoos and shower gels, and plugs for your hair dryer and shaver in all the right places. And there's cable TV, air-conditioning, and a touchtone phone, of course.

Available sports include parasailing, boating, scuba diving, deep-sea fishing, water-skiing, and table tennis. The hotel's 9,000-square-foot sports center is just across the street. Open from 8 A.M. to 10 P.M. every day, it has tennis, squash, and racquetball courts plus an exercise room (and exercise classes, free to guests). At last report, there was no exercise equipment, however, and no sauna or massage available. The 18-hole golf course is nearby.

The 700-room Cable Beach gives you a choice of 11 different places to eat or drink; the most elegant is the fourth-floor Regency Room for continental cuisine by candlelight. The Riviera Room, a bit more casual, is the place for both steaks and seafood. Both are open for dinner only. The King Conch Cafe, opening onto the terrace, is an informal place open 24 hours a day.

Cable Beach Hotel, c/o Wyndham Hotel Company, 5775 N.W. 11th Street, Miami, FL 33126. (305) 262–1397 or (800) 822–4200.

The **Nassau Beach Hotel,** next door, had its heyday in the late '50s and early '60s when the Beatles, Brigitte Bardot, and all the other celebrities of the era stayed here. Thanks to a $7.5-million renovation a couple of years ago, it still holds its own among the big three. Its facade is all new brick, white louvers, and sparkling new "old-fashioned" gas lanterns on the exterior walls.

The guests, mostly couples, range in age from post-pubescent newlyweds to retirees, with a slight emphasis on the latter. If you need an indication that the crowd is somewhat older here, take note that the T-shirts on sale inside say, "My grandma and grandpa went to the Bahamas, and all I got was this lousy T-shirt."

But this is a very pleasant hotel, with a front desk staff friendlier than most in this part of the Bahamas, and 425 attractively decorated guest rooms, every one with an ocean view. The corridors upstairs are so dark you almost need a flashlight to find the keyhole, but the rooms are bright and cheerful. Typical decor includes an abstract design bedspread in tones of rust, beige, and off-white, casual white furniture with mocha accents, and white louvered doors. Sliding glass doors lead to a triangular balcony large enough for two chairs and a tiny table. The bath and dressing room have double basins, good for a couple trying to get ready at the same time. There's a phone, air-conditioning, room service, and a clock radio alarm, but no TV. There is, however, more storage space than you could ever need.

The hotel has three wings, built at different times, but prices ($160–$210) and decor are all the same. The only advantage to the "new" wing (circa 1969) is that the rooms are slightly larger.

The place to swim is the pool, surrounded by off-white beach umbrellas with muted pastel stripes and chaises with matching cushions. The 3,000-foot stretch of beach is fine for sunning, but the area roped off for swimming is barely large enough to get wet.

All the water sports you could want are right here: windsurfing, sailing, snorkeling, paddleboating, parasailing, water-skiing, fishing, and rides in a glass-bottom boat. There are six tennis courts, and other organized activities from volleyball to bingo and backgammon.

The Nassau Beach technically has a health club, located on a lower level of one of the older wings, but it's not what you might expect. The gym (which isn't even free to guests—it's $6 per visit) is smaller than a guest room, with only a few pieces of equipment and weights that guests have to put together themselves. Use of the sauna is $10, and a one-hour massage is $40. Open 9 A.M. –7 P.M., seven days a week.

You can't say the hotel doesn't keep up with the times, however. When they realized the disco craze had cooled, they simply turned their lobby-level nightspot into an exercise studio. Free aerobics classes are held at 9:30 A.M. and 6:30 P.M. five days a week.

And the only nouvelle cuisine restaurant in town is here: Cafe La Ronde, an elegant setting with a full menu of delectable but light French food. Other dinner possibilities here include Polynesian food at Moana Loa, grilling your own steak at The Beef Cellar, or picking your own seafood at the handsomely decorated Lobster Pot.

There are 11 hotel shops, including a liquor store, beauty salon, and small resortwear boutique.

Nassau Beach Hotel National Sales Office, 500 Deer Run, Miami, FL 33166. (305) 871–1830, (800) 223–5672, or (809) 327–7711.

The **Ambassador Beach Hotel** is owned by the same company as the Cable Beach and, according to Wyndham, should be "almost an entirely new hotel" by the 1988 season.

A $4.5-million refurbishment, which began in fall 1986, was scheduled to have been completed by the end of summer 1987. This means new floor coverings, new wallpaper, new chandeliers, and new furniture in both the public spaces and the guest rooms—but no structural changes.

Guest-room rates ($125–$165, single or double) are not expected to go up as a result. In the past, rooms had carpeting, double beds with print spreads to match the draperies, loveseats that pulled out into beds, and sliding glass doors. There were private phones and air-conditioning but no TV.

The pool area was attractive, with dark blue cushions, mauve beach towels, and chunky wood tables and lounges. The pool is just large enough, with landscaping all around, and the beach is quite nice, even though there is limited space for swimming.

By the time of your visit, the Tsunami Restaurant,

with its Polynesian-Chinese menu, will have disappeared and been replaced by the Pasta Kitchen. Expected to stay are the Bunday Bar & Grill, the Flamingo Café, and the Pelican Bar, with its giant TV screen and satellite programming.

The Ambassador Beach has been an attractive, pleasant hotel in the past, but some recent guests have found the hotel run-down, to say the least. Peeling wallpaper, dingy hallways, furniture with broken springs, and woefully inadequate cleaning jobs have been among the complaints. Perhaps this has been a result of keeping the hotel open during refurbishment, perhaps not.

Whatever the case, it will be a good idea to check with your travel agent to be sure the refurbishment is complete and lives up to expectations. If it does, the "new" Ambassador Beach should be more than able to hold its own with its Cable Beach neighbors.

Ambassador Beach Hotel, c/o Wyndham Hotel Company, 5775 N.W. 11th Street, Miami, FL 33126. (800) 822–4200 or (305) 262–1397.

And then there is the **Royal Bahamian,** which began life in the 1940s as a private club (the Balmoral). But the Balmoral became a public hotel in 1967 and was soon outdone by its bigger, more modern neighbors in Cable Beach.

Closed for a $7-million renovation, it reopened in December 1984 as the Royal Bahamian to mostly rave reviews. Most rooms ($160–$180) are in the six-story manor house; the rest are in villas (up to $1,250 per day for the three-bedroom suite). There's haute cuisine at Baccarat's, simpler meals at Café Royale.

The Royal Bahamian, c/o Wyndham Hotel Company, 5775 N.W. 11th Street, Miami, FL 33126. (800) 822–4200 or (305) 262–1397.

When you leave the Cable Beach area, it probably will be for your first shopping expedition downtown. Some of the hotels offer free transportation twice a day or more. Otherwise, you can take a taxi that will cost you $4 or $5 and up. Or meet the Bahamians by taking a public "bus."

The buses, which are actually 10- to 20-seat vans, stop in front of the Cable Beach hotels and take you straight into the Bay Street shopping area for just fifty cents. Remember, they drive on the left here, so when you are going downtown, wait on the same side of the street that the hotels are on.

It's interesting to see the scenery and the glimpses of non-tourist Nassau in between, and to play musical chairs (as the Bahamians politely do for each other) as people get on and off the vehicle. The buses will stop to pick you up almost anywhere. Of course, if you're agile, you can jump on board a moving bus, streetcar-style. But a good place to get one to stop is right in front of the Sheraton.

The **Sheraton British Colonial** is a downtown landmark that, sadly, looks grander from the outside than it really is. Built in the 1920s, it still stands elegantly with its apple-green canopy and pink facade. But inside, there are noisy tour groups checking in and out, and long, dingy corridors upstairs leading to rooms decorated in slightly upscale motel style. We have received so many complaints about this hotel from disappointed guest that regretfully, we cannot recommend it to our readers at this time.

If you want to go sightseeing while downtown, stroll to Rawson Square and hire a horse-drawn carriage for $10 or so an hour. Your horse will trot along the old sections of Nassau, directly behind the bustling shopping area, where old homes (some of them turned into fine restaurants like Graycliff and Buena Vista) are located.

Or if you'd prefer a wider range of sightseeing, hire a taxi driver ($12–$15 per hour) to show you around. You've already seen Prince George Dock and the statue of Queen Victoria downtown; that was Parliament Square. Nearby you'll find the 126-foot water tower, tiny Fort Fincastle, and the queen's staircase.

Sights west of town include Fort Charlotte (built in 1798 and large enough for guided tours) and the upper-crust residential areas of Highland Park, Prospect Ridge, and Skyline Heights.

Fort Montagu, on the other side of the 21-by-7-mile island of New Providence, is a history lesson of two eras.

The fort is from the early 1700s; the now-abandoned hotel of the same name was *the* beach hotel in the 1940s.

Or you can see all of the above on a two-hour guided city and country tour for $11 or so per person. A four-hour city tour ($22 per person) adds the show at Seafloor Aquarium and a Bahamian lunch. Even if you're sightseeing on your own, you can drop by the aquarium for the show, in which trained sea lions and dolphins perform, every two hours. Admission is $5.

Finding interesting tours—from the sightseeing variety to full-day sailing trips or Out Island picnics—is no problem. Your hotel's tour desk will be piled high with brochures and staff members will be eager to book you on one or more outings.

One of the most popular is aboard the *Nautilus,* a 97-foot glassbottom showboat that makes five two-hour cruises per day. Underwater attractions include coral reefs, tropical fish, and even a shipwreck. Then there's the all day Treasure Island trip, a leisurely cruise that drops you off for hours of swimming, sunning, snorkeling, and Bahamian eating, far from the Nassau crowds. If you want to see more of the Bahamas, there are day trips to Freeport and to Harbour Island (off Eleuthera).

PARADISE ISLAND

And then there is Paradise Island. Just cross the bridge on the northeastern side of Nassau ($2 toll for cars, a quarter if you're jogging), and you've arrived in what may be the most active, self-contained resort island in the world. Joseph Lynch (as in Merrill, Lynch) lived here before World War II, when it was still called Hog Island. Then Swedish industrialist Axel Wenner-Gren took over. But development really began in the 1960s, when the company that is now Resorts International got involved.

The only confusing thing about Paradise Island is keeping the names straight. Resorts International owns, among other things, the Paradise Island Resort & Casino. That includes the Britannia Towers Hotel, the Para-

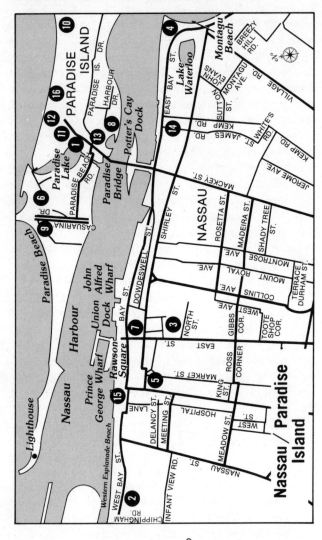

Points of Interest

1) Britannia Towers
2) Fort Charlotte
3) Fort Fincastle
4) Fort Montagu
5) Government House
6) Holiday Inn
7) John Bull
8) Loew's Harbour Cove
9) Paradise Beach Inn
10) Paradise Island Golf Club
11) Paradise Island Resort & Casino
12) Paradise Towers
13) Paradise Village
    Shopping Center
14) Pilot House
15) Sheraton British Colonial
16) Sheraton Grand Hotel

dise Towers Hotel (the two have a total of 1,100 rooms), and the casino that connects them.

The **Britannia Towers** is the more elegant hotel, but not dramatically so. The gleaming lobby, with its marble front desk and columns, brass chandeliers, and light blue walls, is a combination of modern and casual decor. And it is almost always filled with people, activity, and the hum of many voices. Convention groups and dedicated gamblers make up a big part of the clientele.

Within the Britannia, you have four choices of where to stay. There's the North Tower ($170–$300), just five years old, with attractive identically furnished rooms throughout. Among the attractions are blue carpets, bedspreads in a handsome blue seashell-and-net print, closets with sliding glass doors, a mini-fridge, and a wallpapered bath with all the amenities.

Within the North Tower, there is the Paradise Club (floors 9–12). This key club offers private check-in, complimentary continental breakfast in a private 12th-floor room, a rooftop sundeck with hot tub, plus other extras. A typical Paradise Club guest room features two double beds with black-and-white print spreads, a mirrored wall, rose-colored carpet and chairs, sliding glass doors leading to a small balcony, and an attractive bath with a large marble vanity (and little luxuries like complimentary shampoos and conditioners). Rates are slightly higher than those at the rest of the North Tower.

Rooms in the hotel's South Tower (also $170–$300) are larger, if not quite as modern or as luxuriously furnished. Decor includes navy floral print spreads, navy carpet, wallpapered bathroom with phone and fridge, plus balcony. The South Tower was good enough for Howard Hughes, and you can rent his three-bedroom suite (#924, #925, and #926) or any part thereof.

The Britannia also has five villas, each with 16 units. There are no kitchen facilities here. The attraction is being able to walk out your door in the morning and immediately be by the pool or beach. There is only one oceanfront villa, and it costs no more than the others ($225–$250).

This luxury hotel also has what may be the best health club in the Bahamas. The room with hot tub and exercise equipment isn't huge, but it's mirrored, modern, and very attractive. Sauna and massage also are available.

The Paradise Island Resort & Casino is an all-indoor world, if you want it to be. You can walk from the Britannia lobby through an arcade of shops and elegant restaurants into the casino, and from the casino step into the Paradise Towers lobby.

Shops include branches of Mademoiselle (for women's clothes) and Colombian Emeralds, a men's boutique, plus a drugstore and liquor store.

Then you arrive in Birdcage Walk, which is just a circular stopping place with a fountain and a round, rust-striped velvet banquette for drinking, resting your feet, or waiting for your dinner date. Several of the resort's gourmet restaurants surround it.

The restaurants include Villa d'Este, for Italian specialties ranging from veal to pasta; Coyaba, for Szechuan and Polynesian dishes; and the terribly tasteful, somewhat masculine, Bahamian Club for continental and British dishes.

The casino, which is active 24 hours a day, is just ahead. And if you're ever in the mood for breakfast at two in the afternoon or a midnight snack at two in the morning, there's the Café Casino. It keeps gamblers' hours, 11 A.M. to 2 A.M. every day.

If your winnings are impressive, you can stop off in the Crystal Cave and buy a beautiful piece of Lalique or Waterford to celebrate. Then you're on the red carpet walkway into the Paradise Towers lobby, where you can drop into a branch of Greenfire Emeralds if you have any money left.

Paradise Towers' lobby was, until recently, attractive but a little frayed in places. By the time you arrive this season, it should have been doubled in size and completely redone in a tropical-atrium style, complete with fountains and foliage. Guest rooms ($170–$300) are decorated exactly like those in the Britannia's North Tower.

At this writing, dining choices just off the lobby include Gulfstream for seafood specialties and Seagrapes for informal meals—breakfast, lunch, or dinner. The resort's very casual Boathouse restaurant and its very French Café Martinique both are across the street from the Britannia.

Sports? The two-hotel resort has two pools, 12 tennis courts, an 18-hole golf course, horseback riding, and a parcourse jogging trail. There's a three-mile stretch of beach for all water sports, including snorkeling, scuba diving, sunfish sailing, water-skiing, parasailing, windsurfing, and paddleboating.

But the resort doesn't want you to miss the sights. There's a free 45-minute bus tour of Paradise Island twice a day, free bus service over to Nassau's Rawson Square where you can shop, or water taxi service to downtown Nassau for the same purpose.

Paradise Island Resort & Casino, Paradise Island, Bahamas (800) 321–3000 or (305) 895–2922.

The **Sheraton Grand Hotel,** next door, is the new kid on the block and very stiff competition for the well-established hotels. The Grand is certainly the most attractive—and possibly the most courteous—hotel on Paradise Island.

If it's the newest golden boy in the local hotel industry, it lives up to the name literally. The understated, atrium-like lobby is filled with gleaming brass, rose-colored marble, golden-brown tile floors, light golden wood columns, lots of lush greenery around the fountain, and just a touch of red carpet. There are brown sofas, high-backed wicker chairs in the sitting areas, and a handsome lobby bar.

In fact, almost everything here lives up to top aesthetic standards. Le Paon, the island's most fashionable disco, and Julie's, one of the most elegant restaurants here, are as beautifully decorated as they are popular. Even The Verandah, the casual restaurant for breakfast, lunch, and dinner, is much more special than the usual coffeeshop setting. It's an attractive series of rooms with polished bamboo, off-white cushions, and ocean views.

Only the hotel's pool area is undistinguished, but the beach makes up for it.

All guest rooms ($135–$255, single or double) have ocean views. The decor includes double beds with confetti-pattern spreads, floral print dust ruffles, off-white draperies, sliding glass doors leading to a small balcony, and a white louvered double closet with an unstocked fridge inside. The wallpapered baths have large marble vanities and built-in hair dryers. And, of course, there's satellite TV, phone, and air-conditioning.

The 12th floor has been designated the Grand Tier (all rooms $255). Guests here have their own concierge, complimentary Continental breakfast, complimentary afternoon wine and cheese, and little perks like turndown service and toiletries.

If you've saved lots of money for your vacation, rent the Grand's penthouse suite for $11,000 a day. This four-bedroom wonder has its own security desk, an almost nine-foot-long marble bathtub with ocean view in the master bath, gold and marble fixtures, and a hot tub on the living room balcony.

Sports include tennis (four courts), parasailing, windsurfing, and all water sports, which you can schedule at the poolside center. The Paradise Island golf course is nearby.

Lobby shops include branches of Androsia, a liquor store, a florist, and a drug store.

The Sheraton Grand Hotel, Paradise Island, Bahamas. (800) 327–4551 or (809) 326–2011.

The Ocean Club, although a Resorts International property, is as different from the company's two big hotels as night is from day. Set apart from the island bustle, closer to the Versailles Gardens than anything else, this was once the estate of A&P heir Huntington Hartford; a feeling of privacy (not to mention a touch of elitism) remains. There's something more relaxed about this 70-room hotel than its neighbors, too; its PR people like to call it an Out Island atmosphere on Paradise Island.

The people who come here include many New Yorkers, a number of Europeans, and a sprinkling of tennis buffs. They pull into a curving driveway, enter what appears to be a rather grand old home, and sip rum punch while checking in at an antique writing desk. (The night before checkout, the bill will be delivered to their room and later picked up by a concierge.)

Rooms and suites ($135–$500 single or double) overlook the central courtyard, where guests take most of their meals at white wrought-iron chairs under scalloped white beach umbrellas, around a cross-shaped pool and fountain that is surrounded by palms, schefflera, and other greenery.

All guest rooms were upgraded two years ago and now boast mini-bars, bathroom phone extensions, and luxuries from terry-cloth robes to bath gels and shampoos. The baths already were the most luxurious in the Bahamas, with green jungle-leaf wallpaper, dark green tile floors, double basin, makeup stool, toiletries, and a separate WC with bidet. Almost all the guest rooms have balconies.

If you're looking for total privacy, a villa ($700 for two to four people) with a high-walled patio could be the best choice. You get a living room with fireplace and high pine ceilings, two elegant bedrooms and baths, and a kitchenette. Every villa but one has its own hot tub.

The villas are across the way, near the huge pool, nine tennis courts, tennis shop, drugstore, and outdoor lunch restaurant. The Ocean Club's only indoor dining room is used primarily in bad weather. Even afternoon tea now is served in the Courtyard Terrace gardens ($7.50, 3:30–5:30 P.M.).

The real attraction is the ocean. Guests go down wooden steps, stop at the bar for a drink, a big yellow towel, or both, then continue to the clean, attractive (but slightly sloping) private beach. The water is very clear, and guests can reassure themselves that they made the right choice by simply glancing down the way, to the more crowded hotel beaches beyond. All the usual water sports can be arranged here too.

Ocean Club, Paradise Island, Bahamas. (800) 321–3000 or (809) 326–2501.

Club Med, on the other side of Paradise Island, is just as much a world of its own. But oh, what a difference in the mood!

At the front gate, things seem sedate enough. But

stroll through the grounds to the bar overlooking the harbour and you can be almost overwhelmed by the party mood. The friendliness seems quite genuine. The theme song, "Give Me Your Heart," is on the PA system and guests are singing and dancing along.

Club Med is and always has been a one-of-a-kind resort that creates its own environment, taking on only as much of a country or island's character as the natural surroundings provide. Were it not for the beach here and the year-round sun, you could be almost anywhere.

Some of this particular club's acquired assets are the island's most gorgeous stretch of crescent-shaped beach, spectacular grounds, and what may be the largest and best pool at any Bahamian resort. The estate the club is built on belonged to an Olympic swimmer, and she built the pool for her own practice sessions!

The guest register seems to be evenly divided between couples and singles, with a sprinkling of Europeans among the predominantly U.S. crowd. Although a certain amount of topless sunbathing goes on here, Club Med is eager to shed its overly sexy image and is concentrating on sports activities more than ever before.

Tennis is the specialty at this club. You can take advantage of the "Intensive Tennis" program, which gives you three hours of lessons per day (always with the same instructor) plus hours of tennis-related activities. Those include watching video replays of your classes, ball-machine practice, tennis films, and special exercises for limbering up.

If you know John McEnroe only from his TV commercials and think Martina Navratilova is a Russian ballerina, don't let that stop you from visiting this Club Med. Many non-tennis players manage to have a fine time without ever picking up a racket.

Windsurfing is the second most popular sport here. Your other choices of activities (all included in your vacation price) include sailing, snorkeling, archery, yoga, calisthenics, and volleyball.

A one-week vacation costs $920 plus airfare. That includes three meals a day and free wine with every meal except breakfast. This is no small benefit, since Club Med's varied buffets are almost frightening in scope.

Many a first-time guest has put his napkin on the table after a satisfying plateful, only to learn that those were the appetizers. The main courses are set up on another terrace nearby.

Club Med rooms are all doubles. If you don't bring a roommate, they'll find you one. The club's rooms aren't renowned for their luxury or size. A typical room has twin beds and a no-frills bath with shower. No TV or room service, but then no one here spends much time lolling around the room. The disco is always open till 3 A.M. or so.

Call Club Med Sales and Information Center, 3 East 54th Street, New York, NY 10022. (800)528–3100.

The club's nearest neighbor is the **Yoga Retreat,** effectively isolated from the rest of Paradise Island. You can get there by ferry from Nassau or, if you have the energy, you can sneak in the back door by walking along the beach. There are 38 rooms and "beach huts" ($70–$80 MAP).

The dining room serves vegetarian meals only. Although the emphasis here is on yoga, other activities (including tennis and snorkeling) are available and there's a good beach. This is a very casual place—all the better for winding down and coming home rejuvenated, both physically and mentally.

Yoga Retreat, Box N-7550, Nassau, Bahamas. (809) 32–62902. No credit cards are accepted.

Paradise Paradise, on the other side of Club Med, has changed hands and names several times in the last few years. It now belongs to Resorts International again and has undergone a major refurbishment.

The attractive front lawn is still dotted with palm trees and the pool is palm lined. There was no need to improve the beach, which rivals Club Med's as the best on the island. All 100 redecorated guest rooms have terraces and satellite TV. A hotel special offers water sports, tennis, bicycling, and aerobics. Paradise Pavillion, the hotel's new restaurant, offers a very affordable menu.

All along, it's been drawing one of the younger crowds in this area, many in their 20s, perhaps because of the very casual atmosphere and the somewhat lower rates ($120–180 double).

Paradise Paradise, Paradise Island, Bahamas. (800) 321–3000.

The **Holiday Inn** is the last hotel on this side (northwest) of the island, and the pool area is its claim to fame. Despite a private cove, the beach isn't the best in the area, but the huge curving pool more than makes up for it. It snakes around a large deck, dotted with yellow chaises. And there are little footbridges over the pool to and from the thatched-roof snack bar.

This is an 18-floor high-rise of soft yellow stucco, with rows of white iron balconies. The lobby is dramatic, if not sparkling new, with floor-to-ceiling windows (and these ceilings are very high), rust-colored sectional sofas, wicker chairs with modern print cushions, tile floors with rust-colored carpets, and huge floral murals.

As you enter, facing the bar, you'll see an all-American crowd of all ages, probably with their Coke and 7-Up cans right on the tables.

Neptune's Table is the lobby-level seafood restaurant, offering entrees from $9.50 (jackfish) to $20 (*vol au vent,* lobster, or surf & turf), with English trifle for dessert.

An arcade of shops in the rear lobby includes a resortwear shop (heavy on the Androsia), a small jewelry store, a good drugstore, and a video arcade frequented by local teenagers.

Holiday Inn sports include tennis, mini-golf, and all the usual water sports.

Rooms ($155 double) are attractive with carpeting, phones, balconies, and all the familiar comforts you'd expect here.

Holiday Inn, Paradise Island Beach Resort, Box 6214, Nassau, Bahamas. (809) 32–62101.

You can see **Loew's Harbour Cove** from Nassau. It stands alone on Paradise Island's southeastern shore, a tall, modern, white hotel with its own special view of the Nassau harbour.

If the beach matters to you, don't stay here; the beach is a narrow sloping strip of beige sand, facing the harbour. But the pool is just fine, and here is one of the Bahamas' very few swim-up bars. That is, you can enter the section of the pool adjacent to the drink and snack bar, sit on a partially submerged bar stool (water will be over your knees), order your drink and sip it. Wherever you choose to roost, you can watch the Chalk's sea planes take off and land in the water all day.

The lobby is attractive and almost intimate, with rose-pink marble floors, huge potted plants, and recessed lighting. The furniture is a combination of wicker, solid and floral print green fabrics, and wine-red accents. The three lobby shops are branches of Mademoiselle and Colombian Emeralds, plus a combination newsstand/drugstore.

The 250 guest rooms ($125–$165) are sunny and spacious. A typical room has yellow floral print bedspreads, green carpeting, closets with mirrored sliding doors, a framed print that picks up the decor's sunny colors, and a wallpapered bath. Other features include color TV, radio, digital alarm clocks, air-conditioning, and a private phone.

Sports include tennis (two courts, lighted for night play), scuba, snorkeling, sailing, and all of the other usual water sports, plus shuffleboard, paddle tennis, and volleyball. Theme parties (Tuesday night is the Pig Roast Party, complete with fire dance) and special demonstrations are scheduled several days per week. When guests are ready for a change of scenery, it's a short walk to the Paradise Village Shopping Center. The free water taxi can take you right across the harbour to Nassau.

Loews Harbour Cove, Paradise Island, Bahamas. (809) 326–2563.

Paradise Island is not a paradise for sightseers and history buffs. Almost everything here is new and/or part of a hotel complex. But every visitor should see the Versailles Gardens, the 14th-century cloister reconstructed here stone by stone and set in a garden near the Ocean Club. You can thank Huntington Hartford for bringing it over from France.

The 18-hole Paradise Island Golf Club is impressive, and takes up the entire eastern end of the island. But if you're a golfer, you'll see that—as a matter of course.

GOOMBAY SUMMER

Summer 1988 marks the 17th year of Goombay summer. This celebration, originally intended to boost tourism in what was traditionally the slow season, has turned into an island-wide attraction in its own right. The four-month-long (June through September) summer festival offers a full calendar of social, cultural, and sporting events scheduled daily—and repeated weekly for visitors. Celebrations are especially intense in Nassau/Paradise Island, where each hotel sponsors its own beach parties, boat cruises, art fairs, and dances. In Nassau, there are Junkanoo parades, Goombay music festivals, guided walking tours, and tea parties at Government House. Special golf, tennis, squash, and racquetball tournaments abound as well.

Nassau Dining, Shopping and Night Life

Many of your best Bahamian memories will have nothing to do with the beach. One advantage of vacationing in Nassau or Paradise Island is the variety of restaurants, shops, and entertainment available throughout the year.

There are French restaurants, serving caviar and *foie gras;* Italian restaurants that make their own pasta in the back room; and restaurants that have good old American hamburgers and French fries. Above all, there is Bahamian cuisine.

Grouper is often the fish of the day and at its most "native" in the form of grouper fingers (sort of home-fried fish sticks). Conch is on every menu in one form or another. Try conch chowder for a starter, or conch salad for a light lunch. The traditional side dish is peas and rice, and it's delicious, too.

You'll find a restaurant on every corner, and you

could eat very well without ever leaving your hotel's neighborhood. But the three restaurants that now compete for the title of Nassau's best all require a drive or taxi ride downtown. Treating yourself to the very best is the thing to do in Nassau. It's worth the expense and the effort to get there; only in places like these will you find the gracious service that once made this island the coveted retreat of the royal and the rich.

Warning: Ciguatera, a form of food poisoning caused by eating tropical reef fish such as sea bass, red snapper, and grouper, has been reported in the Bahamas. Though this form of poisoning is rare, the only way to avoid it entirely is to abstain from eating tropical reef fish.

THE ELEGANT THREE

Graycliff is a marvelous 240-year-old Georgian Colonial house with a history as intriguing as its menu. The Duke and Duchess of Windsor often played cards here when the house was still the Earl and Countess of Dudley's private home. And although notables from Onassis to the Beatles have enjoyed the hospitality since, manager Enrico Garzaroli remembers Mick Jagger as his most likeable celebrity guest.

The tablecloths here are white crochet-work over solid pink linen and the napkins are edged in old lace; the house even smells the way it should—just the softest hint of must. Guests look out through white louvers to the garden. Or they sit in the garden downstairs, relaxing in summer-striped cushioned chairs, listening to piano music or the fountain splash.

Graycliff is a hotel too, with 14 very elegant rooms renting for $140–$180 per day, but it's far from the beaches and better suited to a rock star in hiding than a vacationer in search of sun.

West Hill Street, opposite Government House, just outside the Nassau shopping district. Telephone 22796. Major credit cards accepted. Lunch and dinner served.

Buena Vista, which wins many votes for the title of Nassau's finest restaurant, has been serving elegant meals for a quarter of a century. You'll enter through a black wrought-iron gate on Delancey Street, move down a small winding driveway, then walk under a maroon canopy into a grand old home. The large air-conditioned dining room, to your right, feels like one in a lovely country inn, accidentally transported from New England and set down in the islands. There's outdoor garden dining, too.

The service is gracious and impeccable, with a setting to match. Mustard tablecloths, wooden floors, hanging plants, and walls of old-fashioned paned windows looking out onto the lawn make for a certain country elegance. The entertainment consists of a male singer whose mood often changes from "Memories" to a double-entendre Bahamian song, then back again.

The wide menu includes Dover sole, steaks, lobster, chicken, and quail, with an average dinner entrée price of $20. There is a special $31 dinner, however, which includes a choice of soup or seafood *coquille*, a salad, and one of six daily specials with vegetables, then a choice of pastries from the fabulous dessert cart plus coffee or tea.

Like Graycliff, Buena Vista is also an inn. But it is in the same neighborhood and not the best base for a sun-and-fun holiday.

Delancey Street, just outside the Nassau shopping district. Telephone 22811. Major credit cards accepted. Lunch and dinner served. Closed Sundays.

Sun And . . . is yet another old Bahamian home turned into a continental restaurant. All the way on the eastern side of the island, past the Nassau shopping district, it's well worth the drive. It has Graycliff's old chef and a fast-growing reputation as one of the town's top three dining spots.

Sun And . . . is formal, but not intimidating. There are flowers at your table and Queen Anne chairs. You enter through an archway then cross over a drawbridge. You can eat indoors or out, perhaps overlooking the greenery-banked pool.

The menu includes rack of lamb or chateaubriand for two, and steaks, veal, and fish dishes. The table is yours for the evening, unlike the policy in some Nassau restaurants where you may be rushed to make way for the next seating.

Sun And . . . is on Lakeview Drive, off East Shirley Street. Telephone 31205. Major credit cards accepted. Dinner only, served Tuesday through Sunday, 6:30–10 P.M. The restaurant is closed in August and September.

FINE HOTEL DINING

There are those nights when eight hours of lying in the sun has been all too much effort, and you can't bear to go any further than downstairs for dinner. These could be the best choices, too, when you just want the finest in food and service.

Julie's at The Sheraton Grand Hotel on Paradise Island started winning culinary stars almost from the day it opened. Low lights and romantic piano music welcome you to its three intimate rooms (plus two private dining rooms on the side).

The mood seems a bit of *la vie en rose,* with pink tablecloths under white lace, Louis XV-style chairs with pink floral print cushions, and pink banquettes along the walls. The food is decidedly French with a Continental accent, from *galantine de canard au poivre vert* or snails in puff pastry to flaming desserts like cherries jubilee and bananas Foster. Entrée prices range from $16.50 (for chicken Gismonda) to $23 for *pres et maree* (that's surf and turf with Bearnaise sauce).

New this year at the Sheraton Grand Hotel is the *Rotisserie.* The only beachfront restaurant in all of Nassau/Paradise Island, this lobby-level dining room features spit-roasted steaks, ribs, fowl, and game (in season).

The Sheraton Grand Hotel, lobby level, Paradise Island. Telephone 62011. Dinner only, 7–10 P.M. seven days a week. Major credit cards accepted.

The Regency Room at the Cable Beach Hotel is very formal (there's a tendency to whisper your order) and in impeccable taste. Everything is burgundy—from the arm chairs, plate trim, and napkins to the orchids in the crystal bud vases on each table. And when you ask for a plain glass of water, you get Evian.

Such good taste is expensive and it attracts as many of the hotel's business visitors as vacationers. Entrée prices start at $19 for baked red snapper in creole sauce to $31 for pan-fried veal with morels and bourbon sauce. Appetizers range from the merely interesting—scallop mousse for $7.50—to the extravagant—Beluga caviar for $55 or *terrine de foie gras de Strasbourg* at $38.

Cable Beach Hotel, fourth floor. Telephone 76000. Major credit cards accepted. Dinner only.

Cafe La Ronde at the Nassau Beach Hotel specializes in nouvelle cuisine, but the setting recalls an almost timeless Paris. Here, behind cafe curtains, beneath an enormous etched-globe chandelier, at rose velvet banquettes along walls of curving mirrors, Toulouse Lautrec might enter at any moment. Or Edith Piaf. Or Leslie Caron as Gigi.

Male diners tend to put on coat and tie for this restaurant, whether they are 21 and honeymooning or silver-haired and here to check on a banking deal.

Entrée prices range from $17 to $25 and include steaks, veal, chicken, and seafood, with many dishes cooked at tableside. Even the fettucine pesto has a light sauce, perfect for vacationers who want to eat well but fit into their swimsuits at the end of the trip.

Nassau Beach Hotel, lower level. Dinner only, 6:30–11 P.M. Telephone 77711. Major credit cards accepted.

Cafe Martinique on Paradise Island seems nothing like a hotel restaurant, but technically it's part of the Britannia Beach/Paradise Towers complex. The striped canopy and the setting here are formal, but the mood isn't.

Whether you eat indoors (in red velvet chairs beneath one of the world's most gorgeous old chandeliers) or out (overlooking Paradise Lake and Nassau's lights across the way), you'll be treated to some of the area's liveliest and best old-fashioned dance music. The mood can switch from Gershwin to Dixieland jazz, depending on exactly what the couples dancing in the moonlight are asking for.

Dinner costs about what you'd expect: from $16.75 for *coq au vin* to $25 for beef Wellington or *langouste*. Grouper amandine, several veal dishes, and filet mignon are also on the menu. For an appetizer, you can blow the budget on caviar or *foie gras* or keep it simple with melon or a shrimp cocktail. The service matches the mood: attentive, but not overly solicitous.

Across the street and down the hill from the Grand Britannia. Paradise Island. Telephone 63000. Brunch and dinner. Major credit cards accepted.

Villa d'Este, just off the lobby of Paradise Island's Grand Britannia Hotel, is a grand high-ceilinged Italian restaurant that makes its own pasta. The setting is classical, with tufted, salmon-colored banquettes and Louis XV-style chairs, a gargantuan Murano-style (but wood!) chandelier, and a huge mural of its namesake, an estate outside of Rome. Entrées start at $14.75 for chicken to $23 for scampi. Other specialties include *saltimbocca, osso bucco,* and a variety of other veal dishes, plus seven kinds of pasta (available either as appetizer or entrée). For the incurably sensible, there's a fruit basket on the dessert cart—right next to the vanilla and chocolate mousses.

Go to Birdcage Walk, between the Grand Britannia lobby and the casino. Paradise Island. Telephone 63000. Dinner only. Major credit cards accepted.

HERE'S TO THE SHOPPERS WHO LUNCH

Virtually every visitor to Nassau spends at least half a day shopping on Bay Street, and eventually most of them get hungry. There are interesting places for memorable lunches in downtown Nassau, but they're tucked away on the side streets, so you must know where to look.

Roselawn is the loveliest. You know you've come to the right place, because 80 percent of your fellow lunch-ers are local businessmen. This makes for an odd juxtaposition of shirts and ties at one table and Bermuda shorts at the next.

The Buena Vista people own Roselawn, and it shows. Beyond the rose-colored canopy, you'll find an almost Mediterranean mood, with archways, carved wood doors, and ceramic tile floors. There's outdoor dining in the garden too.

The service isn't quite up to Buena Vista standards, but neither are the prices. Hot and cold lunch entrées start at $4.75 for a BLT to $14 for a near perfect lobster salad. Homemade pastas as entrées are $7.50. The budget-minded can try the $10 lunch special, which includes soup or salad, the entrée of the day, fruit salad, and coffee.

Roselawn serves dinner, too, with prices ranging from $11 for broiled chicken *a l'Americaine* to $17.50 for charcoal-broiled Bahamian lobster. You can still get the pastas, but they're more expensive at night.

Bank Lane, just past the police station (on your left), off Bay Street. Telephone 51018. Lunch (11:30–2:30) and dinner (6:30–10 P.M.). Major credit cards accepted. Closed Sundays.

The Green Shutters Inn is a popular casual spot for lunch—a touch of Old England in the middle of town. The pub atmosphere includes a fireplace, a dart board, and lots of dark wood. The menu is equally British, with choices like roast beef and yorkshire pudding and steak and kidney pie, as well as local seafood specialties.

Parliament Street, off Bay Street at Rawson Square. Telephone 55702. Lunch (11:30–4) and dinner (6–10:30 P.M.). Major credit cards accepted.

The Terrace is a pleasant, unpretentious place for an outdoor lunch—the only true outdoor restaurant downtown, as a matter of fact. On a hot day, you can be comfortable here under a beach umbrella, a shade tree, or both. There's a small indoor dining room, too, but don't bother. It looks like a Sears Roebuck layout for dinettes.

Separated from the outside world by a stone wall, you can have a big tropical drink in a hurricane glass, then help yourself to the buffet ($6.95). Lunch ordered from the menu could be a steak, seafood, or chicken entrée ($5.50–$12.50), a sandwich ($3–$5), or a Bahamian stew ($5.50).

The Terrace serves dinner, too, with prices ranging from $9.50 (conch curry) to $18 (surf and turf). Specialties include stone crab claws with garlic or mustard sauce, Papa Sam's chicken, and turtle pie. Round it off with English trifle or daiquiri pie for dessert. On Tuesday and Friday nights, there's a Bahamian buffet: all you can eat for $13.95, plus live music.

18 Parliament Street, outside the Parliament Hotel. Telephone 22836. Lunch (12–4) and dinner (6–10:30 P.M.). Major credit cards accepted.

The Cellar lives up to its descriptive name. It's a cool, dark place to stop for a beer or glass of wine on a hot shopping day. You can have a casual lunch, too, in the front room or out back on the garden patio.

The hearty selections include five kinds of pub lunches (perhaps the English pork pie and salad or the Frenchman's platter) for $3.75–$6, plus hot dishes like jumbalaya, lasagna, and stuffed eggplant for $6.50–$8; you'll also find five kinds of quiche priced at $5.75–$6.50.

11 Charlotte Street, off Bay Street. Lunch only. AE and MC accepted for large bills only.

OUT-OF-THE-WAY

The Poop Deck is a casual, ketchup-bottle-on-the-table kind of place overlooking the water. The bar has a low-key nautical feel with lots of boating photos and a "No Opium Smoking" sign on the wall.

A good number of local people and boaters join tourists for relaxed outdoor dining here. Even at dinner, the menu is unpretentious: chicken in the basket, burgers, grouper fingers, and the like. Entrées are $6.75–$15.75.

The lunch menu is similar but cheaper, and everything comes with French fries or Bahamian peas and rice. This is a good spot for lunch when you've been city-sightseeing down this way. It's also a great choice when you want an inexpensive dinner with a view.

Go to East Bay Street, across from the Pilot House, east of the Paradise Island bridge. Lunch and dinner. Major credit cards accepted.

Captain Nemo's is another harbourside restaurant, specializing in seafood and steaks, but closer to town. Go for lunch. You'll find steaks, sandwiches, salads, quiches, and a couple of specials (they change every day—perhaps a choice of baked chicken or minced lobster on Tuesday, or of baked ham or chicken on Saturday). You can watch the Nautilus "surface submarine" tours and the ferry to the Yoga Retreat come and go as you eat.

Deveaux Street, four blocks east of Rawson Square. Telephone 52876. Lunch 12–3 and dinner 6–10 P.M. Major credit cards accepted.

Traveller's Rest just isn't the same since owner/manager Joan Hanna left, but it's still a good spot for a weekday lunch on your way to the airport, or when you're exploring the area near Lyford Cay.

It's an unimpressive white stucco building with an orange roof, set in a grove of palm and sea grape trees, but its unpretentiousness has never bothered its celebrity and tourist clientele. Eat inside on a wooden bench beneath pink-plank shuttered windows and a motley assortment of art or on the patio at picnic tables. The view of blue-green sea is worth any discomfort from heat; anyway, a red Campari umbrella or the waving palm fronds above will help keep you cool.

Everybody orders from the blackboard menu, with changing specials like breaded grouper fingers, conch chowder, pork chops, steamed conch, and curried chicken—all with spicy peas and rice. Lunch with a beer or glass of wine is usually under $10.

Don't arrive for lunch before one, or you might find the place empty. And although the real action is on Sundays when there's live music, the consensus is that there may be a little too much action at times.

Bring your swimsuit. The small white-sand beach across the road is dotted with rocks to stretch out on and the sea is often calm enough to do some swimming.

This is also a good spot to try if you have a mid-day layover at the airport. A $4 taxi ride will bring you here.

West Bay Street, near Gambier. Telephone 77633. Lunch and dinner. AE, V.

CASUAL DINNERS

Albrion's is Nettie Symonette's newest restaurant, located at her Casuarinas Apartments on Cable Beach. The Bahamian/American dinner specialties here include Eleuthera chicken, Inagua pork chops, and Bimini snapper ($10–$16). The lunch menu has more casual offerings, like hot dogs ($3) and cracked conch ($7).

At any time of day, the indoor setting is informal, with tile floors, ceiling fans, mustard yellow tablecloths, hanging plants, and local art. Most of the diners have come here by taxi ($3–$4) from the nearby Cable Beach hotels.

Casuarinas Apartments, Cable Beach, west of the big hotels. Telephone 77921. Breakfast, lunch, and dinner. Major credit cards accepted.

Androsia is in the same neighborhood, and it's a favorite spot for seafood. Their $18.25 dinner special is a buy—featuring a platter of lobster, grouper, conch, and shrimp, with side dishes of peas and rice and vegetables, plus coffee or tea and dessert.

West Bay Street, two blocks past the Cable Beach Shopping Center. Telephone 77801. Lunch and dinner. Major credit cards accepted.

Liz's Steak and Seafood Restaurant is the perfect spot for a late dinner before dancing the night away at the nearby Palace Disco.

It's a pretty little beige house with two floors of dining at brown-clothed tables and bentwood chairs, and an old-fashioned jukebox flashing away downstairs. Dinner entrées ($12–$18) include lobster thermidor, grouper royal (with bananas, herbs, and chutney), scampi, T-bone steak, filet mignon, and surf-and-turf. At lunch, when you may find more local residents than tourists, there's a $3.50 special—or a choice of steamed fish, conch, or chicken ($3.75–$4.50).

Elizabeth Avenue, off Bay Street. Telephone 24780. Lunch and dinner (till 2 A.M.). No dinner service on Mondays. Major credit cards accepted.

The **Corona Hotel Restaurant** looks as though it belongs in a small-town American motel, but the food is locally famous. Brick walls, red tablecloths, and captain's chairs make up the casual decor. Dinner entrées range from $9 for grouper in mustard sauce to $18 for filet mignon. There's a $12 Sunday buffet brunch, served from 11:30 A.M. to 2:30 P.M.

It's on East Bay Street, across from Rubin's. Lunch and dinner. Major credit cards accepted.

Da Vinci, a popular place for dinner, is just outside the Nassau shopping district. Both Italian and French cuisine are served, and the mood is formal enough to require jackets for the gentlemen.

West Bay Street, two doors west of the Sheraton. Telephone 22748. Dinner only, 7–11 P.M. Major credit cards accepted.

SHOPPING

There's no trick to shopping for souvenirs, gifts, and special bargains in Nassau. The stores are all in one area on Bay and its side streets. The salespeople are relatively polite, and prices are marked and firmly set (no haggling, except at the straw market). And almost every store takes at least three major credit cards (usually American Express, MasterCard, and Visa—but Diners Club and Carte Blanche are popular too).

Some items are real buys in Nassau; others are not the bargains they're cracked up to be. But there's never any sales tax, which is a saving in itself. Your best strategy is to make a shopping list ahead of time and check out a couple of prices in your local stores before making the trip. Then decide what you want to shop for here. According to the Bahamas News Bureau, U.S. citizens now can take home $400 worth of duty-free merchandise per person.

Shopping hours are usually 9:00 or 9:30 A.M. to 5:00 P.M., six days a week. A few stores close one afternoon a week, however, so double check if you have a particular item in mind.

Many of the walkways are shaded, so the sun won't cramp your style. Put on your shorts, jeans, or other casual wear (absolutely no swimsuits downtown, please!) and start strolling. Your starting point could be Rawson Square, where the cruise ships come in, right across from the government buildings. Most of the shopping area will be to your right (west), but make a quick left to visit what may be the island's best location for watches and cameras.

John Bull is on the near side of Bay Street, just a block east of your starting point, and it gets all the rave reviews in newspapers and magazines for Nassau's best prices. One entire room is devoted to Rolex, Seiko, Pulsar Quartz, and other watches. Corum and Les Musts de Cartier are in the main room, but a big selection of Canon cameras takes up almost as much space. You'll also find gold chains, other jewelry, and an entire office-supplies shop in the back.

The **Perfume Bar** has several branches in Nassau, including one on Bank Lane. You should be aware that prices for perfume and cologne are fixed in Nassau, so there's no point in wandering through store after store in search of the best buy. Just make sure they have the brand you want.

Leather Masters, a little shop on Bank Lane, could be your next stop. Don't let the forest of Gucci handbags intimidate you. There are very attractive $60 and $70 purses here, too, plus a good selection of belts.

Fashionable resort wear isn't that easy to find in downtown Nassau, but you may find what you're looking for at **Cole's of Nassau,** 10 Parliament Street, particularly if your tastes run toward the preppy. It looks and feels like a friendly small-town dress shop and carries a good selection of sundresses, shorts, nightgowns, lingerie, and shoes. When you've overdosed on Androsia batik, this is the place to come.

The English Shop, on the same block, has a nice antique-shop feel. Beautiful hand-crocheted and embroidered tablecloths are the attraction, but you'll also find English teas, honeys, and a few small antiques.

Colombian Emeralds, on Bay Street west of Parliament, virtually sparkles green with its elegant wares. There are unmounted stones for sale at $300–$3,000 per carat, and even a totally uneducated eye can peer into the display cases and see the difference. Just when you're asking yourself who would come here to buy unmounted emeralds, you notice photos on the wall of U.S. TV personalities—and they're satisfied customers. There are beautiful pieces of emerald jewelry, too, of course, plus watches, lighters, gold gift items, and jewelry made up of other precious stones. If you'd rather pick up a gift of Waterford crystal or Royal Doulton china, walk through the inner doorway to **Treasure Trove** for a fine selection of both.

Pipe of Peace, nearby on Bay Street, sells a lot more than pipes these days. It's really a men's shop, with a selection of watches (Seiko and Citizen), cameras (Nikon and Olympia), stereo components (Aiwa), Dunhill pipes and lighters, and elegant grooming/toiletry kits for travel. The glass antique cars inside glass bottles make nice gifts.

Solomon's Mines, next door, has the kind of gimmicky name some shoppers instinctively don't trust. But give it a chance. It's the only store in town carrying Giorgio cologne—and here it costs $32. There's also a big selection of Royal Doulton and other fine china, too, plus a small selection of Waterford crystal.

Bernard's, also on Bay Street, keeps its best stuff in the back room. There you'll find fabulous Lalique, a lovely selection of Baccarat crystal, and spectacular Baccarat candelabras, starting at $500 or so. There's lots of Wedgwood up front.

Charlotte Street may be the best side street in Nassau for interesting buys, and **Coin of the Realm** is certainly one of its most interesting shops. An armed guard admits you to this small 200-year-old building, where you'll find coin jewelry, escudos, treasure coins, old bank notes, watches, all kinds of jewelry, and antique maps. Stamp collectors can leaf through the offerings (mostly Bahamian), which start at $5 or so, or choose one of the costlier examples ($300 and up) in the display cases. Serious collectors may be invited into the back room, where the selections cost $3000+.

There are two **Brass & Leather Shops** on Charlotte Street, both filled with elegant merchandise. You might choose a Land briefcase for $129 or less, a Gucci bag, a silver flask, an elegant belt or scarf, or almost anything made of English brass or copper.

The Scottish Shop is an unusual and appealing two-floor store, featuring a little of everything from—where else?—Scotland: character dolls from Clark and Vivien (dressed as Rhett and Scarlett) to Charles and Di (dressed for their wedding), Scotch shortbread, Scotch paperweights, and a list of last names, each matched to the appropriate tartan. The tartans themselves, plus sweaters and other clothes, are upstairs.

Balmain Antiques is a second-floor shop on the other side of Charlotte Street, and all too easy to miss. It feels a little more like an art gallery than a retail outlet, but you can find an attractive souvenir to take home and hang on your wall. Framed antique maps are $10–$1700+, matted ship scenes are $50–$200 or so, and framed ship scenes (there are just a few) are only $24–$36. Or you can buy artwork elsewhere and bring it here for custom framing.

The Nassau Shop at 284 Bay Street is the largest store in town and the closest thing you'll find here to department store shopping. The biggest attraction is a huge ground-floor selection of men's sweaters and wool scarves, lots of them from Braemar, and a large selection of cosmetics, Samsonite luggage, and swimwear. Watches include Piaget, Baume & Mercier, and a number of less expensive brands. Closed Thursday afternoons.

The Island Shop, on the corner of Bay and Charlotte, is worth visiting primarily for the second-floor selection of books and magazines. They always seem to have the hot authors' latest, only weeks after the *New York Times* reviews appear—plus art, language, and guide books, and lots of paperback fiction just right for beach and poolside reading.

The Heirloom and **The Porcelain Gallery** are two small sister shops on Frederick Street, both with thick carpets and a don't-touch atmosphere that can be a little off-putting. But the former, where local brides register their china and silver patterns, has lovely selections from Germany. The latter, which carries Wilkens china and silver (also from Germany), could be the place where you'll find the perfect antique to remember this visit by—perhaps a rosewood lap desk, a framed print, a brooch, or pendant. Most of the merchandise is from England.

The Perfume Shop, at the corner of Bay and Frederick, is a pleasant little store with lots of fragrance testers (from Joy to Chanel No. 5). All prices are clearly marked in the display cases. Men's fragrances too.

Old Nassau, also on Bay near Frederick, is a lot larger than its narrow facade would indicate. The front room is owned by John Bull, so you can find the same good prices on watches (Concorde, Seiko, Pulsar, Omega, Ebel, Raymond Weil, Les Musts de Cartier, Corum, Rolex, etc.). The same goes for cameras (Nikon, Canon, Olympus, Konika, Pentax, Hasselblad, Mamiya, etc.). There also are pearls, charms, and other jewelry. The back rooms of the store, not connected with John Bull, include a shoe store, china and crystal shops, and a complete hardware department where you can pick up an ice chest for the picnic.

City Pharmacy, nearby on Bay, is a real hometown drugstore with medicines, greeting cards (the old-fashioned kind), perfumes, and even board games like Monopoly. There's a big suntan lotion selection, and this is one of the few places you *might* find Bain de Soleil without crossing over to Paradise Island.

Carib Jewellers on Bay has a wide selection of Casio watches plus more expensive brands, and a nice selection of German crystal and china in the back. Those glass ships inside glass bottles (same as the glass cars at Pipe of Peace) make nice gifts at $60–$150 or so.

The open-air **Straw Market** is at the corner of Bay and Market, and it's a must for visitors who want to take home one of those colorful hand-decorated straw bags made here. Not to mention similarly designed hats, dolls, and other creations. Be prepared to haggle over price and to pay cash.

Lightbourn's, on Bay between Market and George, is one of the most attractive perfume shops in town, with a large selection of men's and women's fragrances and some pretty atomizers from England, too. All prices are clearly marked in the display cases.

When you reach the Sheraton at the end of Bay Street, go through the entrance to find a small shopping arcade. **Trader Vic's** is the best shop there, but it ought to change its name. It does offer a few Hawaiian shirts, but men's wool sweaters are the attraction here. You might find a real hand-knit Irish fisherman's sweater for under $85 (selling for well over $100 elsewhere in town). The sweaters bear British labels like Dalkeith, Lyle & Scott, and Braemar. And the shop is open on Sundays, which is unusual in Nassau.

It may look as though the shopping district ends here, but Nassau's two best women's boutiques are still to come. Walk about two blocks past the Sheraton to find **Ambrosine** at West Bay and Marlborough. Both local and U.S. customers come here to find fabulous silk (or very good polyester) dresses for special evenings, very fashionable swimsuits (including Ostermans from Israel), and a good selection of sundresses.

Impact is the next store down, and the place to go when you want to add a touch of the outrageous to your wardrobe. If you miss the colorful fashion designers back home, you'll be delighted to find Jeffrey Taylor here, perhaps selling a young customer on a new dress by remarking, "I love the way it makes you walk." There's lots of glitter, sparkle, and sexiness in the clothes here (need a black leather swimsuit with hobnail trim?), but there are quieter garments, too.

If you're staying in one of the large hotels, you could do a lot of your shopping, for both gifts and necessities, right there. The Ambassador Beach has the best drug-store and the Cable Beach the biggest selection, overall, of shops.

Don't expect to do last minute shopping at the Nassau airport. Other than a small selection of perfumes, the best you'll do there is a T-shirt and a bottle of booze.

Most Paradise Island hotel guests take the ferry across to Nassau for at least one Bay Street shopping expedition, but they have their own smaller shopping center just down the street from the Britannia and within easy walking distance of Loews Harbour Cove.

The 11-store Paradise Shopping Center includes branches of John Bull, Mademoiselle, Colombian Emeralds, and Pipe of Peace. Francesca's is one of the nicest shops, with a good selection of sexy Vanity Fair lingerie and nightgowns. You'll also find a deli (the Village Gourmet), a pizza place (Swank Pizza), and a newsstand.

Night life

Both Nassau and Paradise Island take pride in their variety of night life, and there really are choices to suit every taste—although the emphasis is on the noisier variety— from the sounds of steel drums to the constant clatter of the slot machines. So pick a casino, go to a show, visit the local night spots, and get to know the Bahamians. Or just sail away under the moonlight, with a tall, cold Goombay Smash in hand. You can try something new every night, or find a favorite spot and become a regular during your stay.

The casinos are Nassau's best-known night spots, and the **Paradise Island Casino** began it all. Thanks to a $1.5-million renovation in 1984 and an expansion last year, the 20,000-square-foot casino is more glamorous than ever with a mirrored ceiling, a $50,000 chandelier made of brass palm leaves, Doric columns, and a new coral, green, and white color scheme. Actually, the casino can provide both daytime and nighttime amusement. The blackjack and craps tables open at noon, and the slot machines (all 1,000 of them) are available 24 hours a day. But it's at night that the casino goes into full action, adding tables for roulette, Big Six, and baccarat.

And at night, it's on with the show. You can see Paradise Island's 90-minute casino production, *Dazzling Deception,* as a dinner show or later in the evening with only drinks served. If you're staying at the Paradise Island Resort on its Gourmet Dining Plan, the show is free.

Be prepared for glitter, because that's all this show is about. It opens with a bare-breasted blonde in a tiara, glittered bikini, and ostrich plumes, descending in a gilded cage. The evening's first magic trick is turning a dog into a scantily clad dancing girl. And we later get to see a live tiger, panther, and (caged) lion on stage.

But the costumes are spectacular, the British comedian is likeable, some of the acrobatic dancing very impressive, and there's some very clever use of film— with live performers appearing to walk in and out of the on-screen action.

The casino is located between the Grand Britannia and Paradise Towers hotels, and can be reached by walking indoors through either of the lobbies. For show reservations, call 63000. Back in the U.S., call (800) 321–3000.

The **Cable Beach Casino,** located at Nassau's hotel of the same name, is a relative newcomer to the gambling scene here—but the developers knew exactly who they were competing with when they designed it. It was designed to match the original Paradise Island facility, point for point.

Its 20,000 square feet contain 44 blackjack tables, six for craps, four for roulette, one for baccarat, and 526 slot machines. There are 300 croupiers, all women. And if you're truly a small-time gambler, you could be happy here: there are nickel slot machines.

Its casino shows have been winning rave reviews too. A recent one was *Les Fantastiques*, which had the good taste to use Gershwin music to set a certain mood for its incredibly expensive sets and leggy showgirls. There are shows at 9 and 11 P.M. Tuesday through Sunday. For reservations or information, call 76200. Tickets were recently priced at $28, $22, and $15, but call for updated information.

To find the casino, just walk through the Cable Beach Hotel lobby and past its indoor shopping arcade.

DANCE THE NIGHT AWAY

If you're looking for the most fashionable and glamorous disco in town, you'll find it at the Sheraton Grand Hotel on Paradise Island. **Le Paon** (the peacock) is the island's "in" spot, a title it could have won on looks alone. It's located at the back of the Grand's lobby, behind double glass doors. There are green plants in gleaming brass tubs, an entryway floor of red bricks in concentric circles, two huge round mirrors in back with stylized peacock heads etched in white, a handsome bar to the right, tiny glittery golden lights, and a sunken dance floor. There are both banquettes and tables in the main room. If you have a touch of romance in your soul, however, head straight for the back room with its gorgeous picture-window view of the beach.

Happy hour at Le Paon is 5–9 P.M. After nine, dress up a little to enjoy the lively hours ahead.

On the other hand, if you asked Nassau residents themselves to name their favorite spot for late-night dancing, they'd probably name **The Palace Disco** on Elizabeth Avenue, just off Bay Street. It draws a mixed crowd of Bahamians and tourists, and goes strong Tuesdays through Saturdays from 9 P.M. until four in the morning.

The decor is disco-modern, with vertical mirror

strips at the entrance, brown and chrome chairs at wooden tables, and a railing separating the smallish, round dance floor from the horseshoe-shaped bar and the rest of the room. There's an upstairs balcony with a bar, mostly with tables for two overlooking the action. Both disco and live music are part of the scene every night. Telephone 57733.

Ronnie's Rebel Room is the place to go when you're in the mood for all of those island attractions you went on vacation to see. You'll find a limbo dancer, a fire dancer, a steel drummer, and some Calypso revival singers here, just outside the Nassau shopping district. However, there are only three nights a week to choose from so plan ahead. Shows are held Wednesdays and Saturdays at 8 and 10:15 P.M., and Tuesdays at 10:15 only.

It's on West Bay Street, next to the Atlantis Hotel. Telephone 34483. Reservations are recommended.

The Grand Hotel also features a typically Bahamian show, **The Junkanoo Revue,** on Wednesday nights. Sabu the Great, an authentically costumed voodoo dancer, stars in this panoply of glass-eating, fire dancing, limboing, and steel band music. Come for a barbecue dinner at 7 P.M. ($25) or for the show alone at 8:15 ($15, which includes two drinks). Telephone 62011, extension 667.

Other night life possibilities include **Peanuts Taylor's Drumbeat Club** and its nightly Afro-Bahamian Revue (West Bay Street, telephone 24233) and live music at **The Back Room** disco (Balmoral Beach Hotel, Cable Beach, telephone 77481).

MOONLIGHT CRUISES

If your idea of a perfect evening is something quieter, why not take a romantic moonlight cruise? The **Nautilus Dinner Cruise** takes you out on the 97-foot glass-bottom boat at 7 P.M. any evening Monday through Saturday. Thanks to the powerful underwater lights, you'll be able to see all the colorful marine life as you float along. This tour leaves from the New Mermaid Marina at the corner of Bay and Deveaux streets, next to Captain Nemo's restaurant. Telephone 52871 for reservations and current prices. Or make arrangements through your hotel's tour desk.

Perhaps even more romantic is the **Wild Harp Sunset Dinner Cruise** aboard an elegant 56-foot sailing schooner. You'll leave at 6 P.M. from the Nassau Yacht Haven (or at 6:15 from Loew's Harbour Cove Hotel, if you're staying on Paradise Island), then sail into the sunset with the lights of Nassau Harbour and its huge cruise ships as your backdrop. The tour price ($40 with round-trip transfers, $35 without) includes the three-hour cruise, a buffet dinner under the stars, a welcoming cocktail, one complimentary glass of wine with dinner, and live music. There's a cash bar for any additional drinks you want to order. Telephone 21149 (daytime) or 41206 (at night), or make reservations at your hotel's tour desk.

Local tour companies also offer a variety of night club, cabaret/casino, and pub-crawling tours on certain nights. Prices range from $17 to $47 per person. For Tropical Travel Tours (Gray Line), telephone 24091; for Curtis Brothers Travel & Tour Company, telephone 35977.

Freeport/Lucaya

If tourism seems well-developed here, it was planned that way. In 1964, there were eight hotel rooms on Grand Bahama Island. Today there are more than 3,500, and its capital, Freeport/Lucaya, is the Bahamas' second largest city.

Chances are, you'll arrive at the Freeport airport and taxi (about $4) to the Princess or Princess Tower hotels, which are across the street from one another. And until you want to go to the beach, everything you'll want to see is right here: the casino, the International Bazaar, and the restaurants—all owned by Princess International.

The **Princess Country Club** is the garden property, with its manicured lawns separated from the sister hotel by a four-lane street and a pedestrian walkway. This low, rambling building is the older of the two, but has undergone refurbishing in recent years. The rather formal

60

royal blue and ivory lobby has stayed the same, but almost everything else has been changed.

The pool area is something special, with waterfalls
and a Jacuzzi set among artificial rock formations. The
open-air poolside restaurant, John B., has been redone
with thatched roof, ceiling fans, and lots of greenery.

The Princess' rooms ($110–$125 double) were set
up motel style, and the decor will depend on which wing
you end up in. Ask for something in the renovated 700
Wing. You'll find two double beds with rattan head-
boards and peach print spreads, matching draperies,
beige carpet, a closet with sliding mirrored doors, a wallpapered bath with a marble vanity, cable TV, and direct-
dial touchtone phone.

Actually, the 900 Wing is the deluxe area—it has
larger rooms and separate dressing areas outside the
baths. They're attractive, but probably won't be renovated by the time you arrive.

Guanahani's is the glamour restaurant at the Princess. It's a separate little house with a glass wall overlooking the pool (so you can watch the last sunbathers),
bleached wood walls, rattan chairs with dark green or soft
coral batik cushions, lots of lush potted plants, brass
ceiling fans, and huge chandeliers. Dinner ordered from
the menu ($14.25–$18.25) includes salad, bread, vegetables, and dessert as well as Bahamian-style main courses
like orange marmalade chicken and papaya ginger pork.

The hotel also boasts a golf shop and The Rib Room
restaurant, best known for great steaks.

The 10-story **Princess Tower,** built in 1970, attracts
the high-rollers, conference groups, and an urban East
Coast crowd. A great deal of it was redecorated as part
of a recent multimillion-dollar refurbishment, but standard rooms are still only $110–$125. Expect to find the
little luxuries, as well as cable TV, telephones, and air-
conditioning. And if things have gone according to plan,
the ninth and tenth floors have been turned into a "towers" section, with concierge, private check-in, a breakfast
room, and other extras.

The service is unusually gracious.

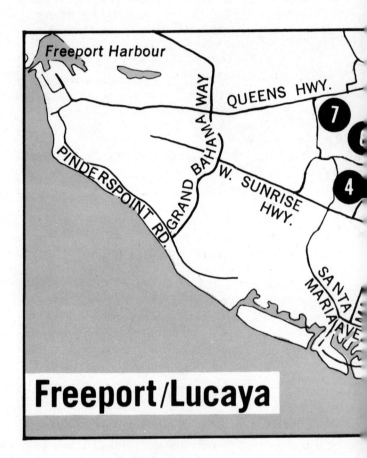

Freeport Harbour

QUEENS HWY.

GRAND BAHAMA WAY

PINDERSPOINT RD.

W. SUNRISE HWY.

SANTA MARIA AVE.

Freeport/Lucaya

Points of Interest

1) Atlantik Beach
2) Freeport International Airport
3) Holiday Inn

4) International Bazaar
5) Lucayan Genting
6) Princess Casino
7) Princess Tower Hotel

Princess Country Club, Box F-2623, Freeport, Grand Bahama. Princess Tower, (809) 352–6721. Princess, (809) 352–6721.

The Casino, next door, was completely refurbished in 1986. You'll find a handsome new circular bar overlooking the action, the rather formal Crown Room gourmet buffet restaurant, the casual Garden Cafe (open till 4 A.M. for hungry gamblers), and a $100,000 jackpot. Amusements include blackjack, roulette, and, of course, slot machines.

Soiree, the glittery casino show, manages to charm almost everybody at one point or another. Nightly at 8:30 and 10:45. A $20 ticket includes two drinks and gratuities. (809) 352–7811.

Xanadu Beach & Marina Resort, Freeport's only major beachside hotel, reopened in December 1985 with a variety of accommodations. Guests can choose from rooms in the 12-story tower, the pool wing, or the two-story villas. Room rates are $105, and villas, accommodating up to six people, $375–$1,000.

There's tennis, on-site water sports, pool, sauna, and a marina. Restaurants include the Persian Room for French food and the Escoffier Room for a variety of cuisines. And, as the management likes to point out, the casino isn't far away.

Xanadu Beach and Marina Resort, P.O. Box F-2438, Freeport, Grand Bahama. (800) 222–3788 or (809) 352–8720.

Of course, when you've won all that money at the casino, you'll want to spend it at the 10-acre **International Bazaar.** Enter through the red-lacquer Japanese gate several yards down the way, or just keep walking past the

Princess Tower and past the casino, then slip right into the first pavilion. There are dozens of stores (representing a total of 25 countries) and every visitor should schedule at least half a day to stroll through them, even if only to window shop. If the settings look as though they're straight out of the movies, they almost are. The whole thing was designed by a Hollywood special effects man, and built in 1967 at a cost of $4 million.

The stores all accept major credit cards. You'll find a map posted at the entrance; in alphabetical order, here are some shops to check out.

Androsia of Lucaya is just that—a big selection of Androsia batik fashions, made in the Bahamas. Garments include sundresses, bikinis, tube tops, skirts, and culottes.

Bahama Coin & Stamp Ltd. is a tiny shop worth looking into, whether you're a collector or an amateur looking for an unusual souvenir. On the cheap side, there are coin sets for as little as $5, uncirculated Bahamian three dollar bills for $5.95, and a set of four Churchill stamps for $5. Then there are more elegant items, like the Krugerrand money clip ($1175) and the Bahamian $100 gold piece ($650). There are Roman coins from 350–530 A.D., too.

Colombian Emeralds is a bigger, friendlier store than its branch in Nassau. The unmounted emeralds, amethysts and other stones are in a separate room. A variety of merchandise, including coral jewelry, pearls, and watches, are in the main room.

Gemini I, where rock music always plays in the background, is a boutique for the young and modern, featuring shoes, belts, casual jewelry, and all kinds of accessories. Look for the great collection of evening bags in all kinds of fabrics and styles.

Ginza appears to be the place to buy a watch, thanks to what may be the lowest prices in town on Seiko, Citizen, Pulsar Quartz, Rolex, Les Musts de Cartier, Piaget, and more. A good selection of cameras, a separate room of Mikimoto pearls and other jewelry, plus a friendly, helpful sales staff make this store a must during your visit.

The **Island Galleria** used to be an art gallery, and

there are still some watercolors and prints for sale in the back (most in the $100–$500 range). Up front, it's now a very classy, spacious store with a good selection of jewelry, watches, china, and Waterford crystal.

Leather & Things has briefcases, picture frames, backgammon sets, purses, luggage, desk sets, and even elegant tool kits in leather. A handsome store, although the bargains may not be as great as they're cracked up to be. A briefcase that was $129 in Nassau was only $5 less here.

The **London Pacesetter Boutique** is a small corner shop with large possibilities. Merchandise includes fashionable Gottex swimsuits, some trendy resortwear, and a selection of English sweaters with all the right labels.

Midnight Sun has two stores, both with lovely merchandise from Scandinavia and elsewhere. The first is the most formal, with frosted Finnish glass, Lalique figurines, and Baccarat glassware. The second, catty-corner from the first, carries everything from Johnson Brothers ironstone to brightly colored hair combs from Copenhagen.

The **Old Curiosity Shop** is an attractive and tasteful shop, specializing in both antique and reproduction jewelry. Brass, copperware, silverplate, and clocks sell well, too. Most of the things are from England, but some have come from France, Germany, or Holland.

Scandia Solomon's Mines is worth a visit, if only for the selection of Waterford crystal.

Tivoli is a very chic little Scandinavian store with all sorts of ordinary items made special by Danish design: housewares, games, jewelry, clothing, candles, etc.

There's a straw market at the far end of the International Bazaar, where you can buy locally made bags, hats, and the like. Walk by fast if you're not interested; the sales pitch can be presented insistently.

There are any number of places to stop for a meal during your shopping spree. Some of the most interesting include the following international spots:

The **Japanese Steak House** and Tea Garden, next to Ginza, serves an outdoor lunch 11:30–3:30 and dinner from 5:30–10:30 P.M. A large green Buddha welcomes you at the top of the stairs. Eating outdoors is the most fun. Although you'll sit at very un-Japanese orange plastic chairs, you can look down on Asia to your left and on the boulevards of France to your right.

Michel's, a sidewalk cafe on Place des Wallons, serves both lunch and dinner underneath blue and white umbrellas, on wine-label-design tablecloths. Dinner entrées, served 5–11 P.M., include red snapper *beurre noisette* and *entrecote cafe de Paris* ($7.50–$13.50). During the day, have something more casual: deep-fried shrimp at $5.50, or half a papaya filled with chicken salad for $3.50.

Rendezvous is another outdoor cafe, just down the boulevard in "France." You can get sandwiches, burgers, and light lunch platters during the day. At night, there's a real bargain: a $4.95 steak dinner, available 7–8 P.M. and again between 10 and 11. Drinks are $.99 at various Happy Hours during the day. The setting is very Parisian, with red, white, and blue umbrellas and lacy white wrought-iron chairs.

The **Sir Winston Churchill Pub** is at the very end of the Bazaar, across the street from the straw market. This is a true meeting place at any time of day (open 11 A.M. –2 A.M.), perfect if you want to make new friends in Freeport. You can eat in the garden or in the cozy publike dining room. Choices range from fish and chips to six kinds of pizza, and from cracked conch to broiled lobster, with entrées priced from $3.50 to $17.50.

The pub itself is quite large, with banquettes and chairs in that dark, faded green you've seen in libraries and university clubs. Houndstooth wallpaper, ceiling fans, pawn-shop-globe light fixtures and photos of both

Churchill and the queen complete the authentic British mood. But there's a jukebox playing loud rock in mid-afternoon, and the nights with live music are the best meeting times.

If you're in the mood for another helping of British food go to **Pub on the Mall** the next day. Open for both lunch and dinner (till 5 A.M.), this stone and cross-timber building across the street from the International Bazaar is a popular late-night gathering place, too. Menu choices include steak and kidney pie, $4.95; Welsh rarebit, $3.95; and fish and chips, $7.95.

When you want a special dinner outside the hotel complex, **Ruby Swiss** is the place to go. Near the golf course and just a short taxi ride from the Princess Hotels, this unimposing restaurant in a former private home is considered Freeport's best by many people. The setting is more casual than the ads indicate, with red napkins, blue tablecloths, beamed ceilings, tall windows, and live music every night. There's even a tiny dance floor.

The Ruby Swiss menu is extensive. Swiss specialties include *zuercher geschnetzeltes* (veal in wine sauce with *roesti*), *schafhauser sauerbraten* (a braised beef with red cabbage), *Engadiner goulash, wiener schnitzel,* and *fondue bourgignon,* not to mention seafood choices from conch to lobster thermidor. Entrée prices range from $12.75 to $19.

The crowd is mostly couples, with a well-scrubbed middle-America look (men in short-sleeved knit shirts, women in casual skirts and blouses). Best time to go: sunset. The blue-gray sky against tall pines afterward makes a perfect dinnertime view. Telephone 352–8507.

Pier I is for the night you want a real seaside atmosphere. This little wooden house is built on stilts right in the water of Freeport Harbour. The mood is casual, with a fabulous sea view and refreshing ocean breeze. Seafood is the specialty. Telephone 352–6674.

To get there, take West Sunrise Highway through the industrial section. When the road ends, make a left and follow the Freeport Harbour signs. At the green and white restaurant sign, turn right. Don't worry about getting home: This is where cruise ships come in, and a line of taxis is usually waiting.

The **Captain's Charthouse Restaurant** is the place for steak, but don't expect a romantic view—it's right on the highway. Just take West Sunrise until you see the restaurant sign, and the two-story brown wooden building on your right. Open for dinner only (5–11 P.M.), this restaurant offers special prices that start at $5.95 if you eat early (5–6:30 P.M.). Other specialties include lobster, prime ribs, and live Calypso dinner music. Telephone 373–3900.

The **Stoned Crab** could be a beach house that belongs to a well-to-do friend. It seems to be nothing but pointed thatched roofs and glass, with a huge fig tree out front and the beach out back. Eat indoors on small wooden tables and captain's chairs, with a view of palm trees and beach, or take a table on the patio out back. You're on the beach. You'll find American and Bahamian specialties on the menu. Telephone 373–1442.

To get there, take East Sunrise to Sea Horse Road to Midshipman Road. Turn right at the old stone sign that has letters missing and now says "rtun marind". You'll cross a little bridge and see the restaurant signs.

This is the beach at Lucaya, and here you'll find how the other half lives on Grand Bahama Island. While the gamblers and the sophisticates are in Freeport, Lucaya draws a younger, more active, more casual crowd—including the beach bums and the divers—taking advantage of inexpensive vacation packages.

The **Holiday Inn** is one of the area's top gathering places. Its lower-level disco, Panache (formerly The Tipsy Turtle), draws both singles and couples. If there's a place to make new friends, it's here among the salmon-pink leather banquettes and rattan chairs. The $8 cover charge includes two drinks. Open 9 P.M.–3 A.M. Telephone 373–1333.

The hotel itself is a modern white structure, right on the beach. The low-lighted, marble-floored lobby has intimate conversation groupings of blue print sofas and

is surrounded by shops, including a branch of Mademoiselle and a liquor store. The lower-level exercise center
isn't huge, but has a mirrored wall and gym equipment.
Regular exercise classes are held here. Other features
include three restaurants, pool, tennis, golf nearby, and
all water sports. ($96–$132).

There are three types of rooms. The beachfronts
have a king-sized bed, carpet, color TV, and a balcony.
If you want a walk-in closet, ask for one of the corner
beachfront rooms. The deluxe rooms have two double
beds, a balcony, and a view of the pool. Superior rooms,
which really are the hotel's standard offering, may overlook the garden or the roof of the hotel. If the view
matters to you, ask first.

Holiday Inn/Lucaya Beach, Box F-2468, Freeport,
Grand Bahama. Telephone (809) 373–1333.

The **Atlantik Beach Hotel,** the Holiday Inn's next-
door neighbor, was recently renovated. Changes include
a refurbished lobby, library, and shopping arcade, the
Butterfly Brasserie coffee shop, and Alfredo's Restaurant
for Italian cuisine.

Room rates are $95–$140 double, $105–$150 for
suites, and a concierge floor—the Corona Classic Club—
has been added.

Hotel guests have access to tennis courts, a large
rectangular pool, an excellent beach, and windsurfing.

Atlantik Beach Hotel, Airport Executive Tower #1,
1150 N.W. 72d Avenue, Miami, FL 33126. Telephone
(800) 622–6770 or (305) 592–5757.

The **Genting Lucayan Beach Resort & Casino**
opened its doors in 1986. The oceanside main hotel went
into operation, complete with casino, restaurants, bars,
pool, theater, cabaret, guest rooms ($110), and the Lanai
Wing offering concierge service ($180).

By the time you visit, the 150-slip marina and a 168-
room second hotel (the redone Lucayan Bay) will be
completed and in full operation. The resort's on-premise
activities include deep-sea fishing, windsurfing, sailing,
tennis, glass-bottom boat tours, and scuba diving.
UNEXSO (Underwater Explorers Society) is also here,
offering a variety of complete diving vacations.

Genting Lucayan Beach Resort & Casinos, Box F-

336, Lucaya, Grand Bahama. (809) 373–7777 or (809) 373–1225.

The entire island of Grand Bahama is almost 100 miles long, and the West End district is a good 25 miles from the casino and bazaar. Here you'll find **Jack Tar Village,** a 2,000-acre resort run very much like Club Med. Pay $160 single or $260 double per day, then relax: Everything is included. That means all meals, unlimited liquor (even Club Med doesn't offer that), unlimited wine with meals, tennis, golf, water sports, entertainment, and all other activities. There's a saltwater pool, a beach, marina, shopping arcade, and disco. The only thing you'll have to pay extra for is your golf cart. Even a midnight snack is part of the package.

Jack Tar Village, 403 South Ackard, Dallas, TX 75202. Telephone (800) 527–9299 or (809) 346–6211.

The only other reason most visitors to Grand Bahama drive west is to visit the **Buccaneer Club** for drinks, dinner, and the seaside atmosphere. The best way to go may be to take a tour. Local tour operators offer a Buccaneer Club beach party at least twice a week. The $25 price tag includes an open bar (for one hour), appetizers, dinner, transportation, and tips.

Harry's American Bar, another popular but out-of-the-way spot for drinks and dinner, is right down the way.

The large, well-known resorts aren't your only accommodation choices on Grand Bahama. A number of smaller hotels, most with air-conditioned rooms and all with at least one swimming pool, offer a variety of atmospheres for a vacation here. All rates listed are per room, double occupancy, for the winter season. Reservations can be made directly with each hotel or through the **Bahamas Reservation Service,** (800) 327–0787. The list of smaller hotels includes the following:

Castaways Resort, 136 rooms and 1 suite, near the International Bazaar and Princess Casino, $58, (809) 352–6682.

Channel House Resort Club, 19 apartments, each

with full kitchen, in Lucaya, about 150 yards from the beach, $65, (809) 373–5405.

Coral Beach Hotel, a 10-unit apartment hotel right on the beach, $60, (809) 373–2468.

Freeport Inn, 170 rooms, many with kitchenettes, near both the bazaar and casino, $47–$69, (809) 352–6648.

New Victoria Inn, 40 rooms, scuba diving instruction available, $45, (809) 373–3040.

Silver Sands, 144 studios and 20 one-bedroom suites, less than 100 yards from beach, $75–$105, (809) 373–5700.

Windward Hotel, 100 rooms (including some suites), near the bazaar and casino, $58–$66, (809) 352–8221.

Organized tours can be the best way to enjoy the watery side of Grand Bahama, particularly if you're staying in downtown Freeport, and they're the best way to see the sights. Possibilities include a city bus tour that visits Garden of the Groves (a 12-acre botanical garden), the sunset booze cruise or wine & cheese cruise, a deep-sea fishing trip, trimaran sailing, glass-bottom boat trips, and scuba diving tours. Prices range from $10 to $60 per person. Check with your hotel for further information.

Getting to Freeport/Lucaya is the easiest part of your vacation. Several major airlines fly here from U.S. cities, and Bahamasair has frequent service from Nassau.

Unless you plan a lot of exploring, your own two feet and an occasional taxi are all the local transportation you'll need. If you want to rent a car and see Grand Bahama on your own, Avis, Budget, Dollar, and National are among the rental companies at the Freeport airport.

Eleuthera and
Harbour Island

The sand really *is* pink in Harbour Island, but you have to take a close look to tell. When you do, you'll see tiny grains of pink coral sparkling in the sun.

Technically, Harbour Island isn't even part of Eleuthera. Yet this two-square-mile island off the larger island's northern coast has become the center of Eleutheran tourism.

After your flight to North Eleuthera, take a taxi to the ferry. About seven dollars later, you'll find yourself in 300-year-old Dunmore Town, just minutes away from your hotel. Several of your choices are lined up on the northern beach.

Pink Sands was established a long time ago, when rich people still vacationed by going away to "camp"— resorts of rustic stone cabins with forest-like grounds,

73

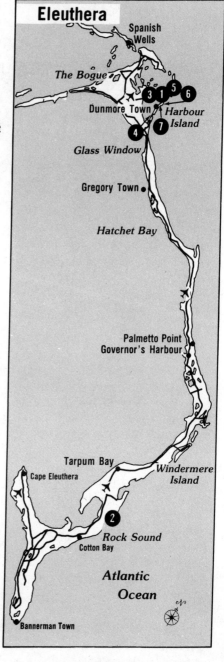

Points of Interest

1) Coral Sands Hotel
2) Cotton Bay Resort
3) Dunmore Beach Club
4) Ocean View Club
5) Pink Sands Hotel
6) Romora Bay Club
7) Valentine's Yacht Club & Inn

lots of privacy, and lots of cachet. Many of today's guests (average age 40+) have been coming since then.

Pink Sands is a little old-fashioned, but that's the essence of its charm. Men wear coats and ties to dinner. The dinner music is a non-amplified Calypso band. And the staff will still come to your cottage and prepare breakfast in your own kitchen. The cottages ($260, Full American Plan) have ceiling fans and sliding glass doors leading onto the patio. There's no air-conditioning, but the ocean breezes feel just wonderful. Tennis and water sports are available.

Pink Sands, Box 87, Harbour Island, Bahamas. (809) 333–2030

The **Coral Sands Hotel,** just down the beach, is a much more informal, action-oriented resort. There are 33 rooms ($105) (air-conditioned during the summer), tennis, water sports, and a dining room with Bahamian cuisine. Closed September through mid-November.

Coral Sands Hotel, Harbour Island, Bahamas. (809) 333–2350.

At the **Dunmore Beach Club,** the same people come back year after year, often making reservations at checkout time. You can see the resort's hillside white gazebo from the beach. A closer look reveals the hotel's charm: lots of white wicker, greenery and yellow accents, one- and two-bedroom cottage units with patios, and what even the competition admits is the best food on Harbour Island.

There are six cottage buildings, accommodating 28 guests ($190 double, Full American Plan). It's usually closed May through August.

Dunmore Beach Club, Box 122, Harbour Island, Bahamas. (809) 333–2200.

The **Ocean View Club** has only eight rooms (every one different), a youngish clientele, and a lobby that seems like a cheerful living room, with its piano, fireplace, plank ceilings, and small alcove bar. Every room ($90) has one thing in common: an ocean view.

Ocean View Club, Box 134, Harbour Island, Bahamas. (809) 333–2276.

Romora Bay Club, on the eastern end of the island, has the loveliest grounds of any Harbour Island resort.

Terraced gardens lead from the main building to the waterfront and bayside bar.

The main house lobby is very attractive, with its fireplace, almost formal blue and white furniture, baby grand piano, and black-and-white checkerboard tile floor. Whether you stay here or elsewhere, it's a lovely place for dinner. Ask to sit in the front room, with its white, country-European feeling.

Rooms ($111–$146) are in air-conditioned villas. There's a strong emphasis on water sports here, including sailing trips, boat rentals, and complete scuba diving package vacations.

Romora Bay Club, Box 146, Harbour Island, Bahamas. (809) 333–2325, (305) 287–8293, or (800) 327–8286.

Valentine's Yacht Club & Inn is right downtown and anything but secluded. Many of the guests at this friendly hotel are divers (its own dive center is across the street); many others are the owners of boats docked at its new 33-slip marina. Valentine's newest attraction is its harbor-front bar, The Reach.

The motel-style rooms ($90–$100) have queen-sized bed, carpeting, and sliding glass doors. There's no room service, but they say a neighbor (known as Friendly Willy) will give you some fresh fruit from his yard for a dollar, if you walk outside your room and call his name.

The pool and hot tub are just outside the main building. This side of the island is beachless, but Valentine's has its own Dunes Club on the northern shore.

Valentine's Yacht Club, Box 1, Harbour Island, Bahamas. (809) 333–2142, (809) 333–2080, or (305) 491–1010.

Telephone service to Eleuthera is not always the best, so you may want to write for reservations instead.

The hotels have very strict meal hours, but you can eat at almost any time of day (well, until 9 P.M. or so—Harbour Island closes early) at **Angela's Starfish Restaurant** downtown. Just go into the aqua stucco house, choose your entrée from the lengthy Bahamian menu (emphasis on seafood, of course), place your order at the window, then choose one of the small white tables or picnic tables outdoors. A delicious, home-cooked meal will soon be placed before you. (809) 333–2253.

George's, the island's late-night spot of choice, looks a little like a private home turned roadside diner. It welcomes a crowd that's usually half tourists and half locals for live music and general hanging-out until 2 A.M. or so. For special events, there's a cover charge (usually $4). This is the kind of place in which the noise level during a swimsuit fashion show rivals that at the average rock concert. To find George's, take the first right (going toward town) after Valentine's. Two more rights, and you're there.

Vic-Hum's (pronounced wick-ums, Bahamian style) is the island's other late-night choice—you'll find fewer tourists there.

Many visitors also take day trips, by private boat or the local ferry, to Spanish Wells. It's a sparkling clean little fishing community that looks even more authentically New England than Harbour Island. Bonus: There are lots of straw goods that make great gifts and souvenirs.

Seeing the rest of Eleuthera while staying in Harbour Island is not quite as easy. This island is so long and narrow that it has three airports.

One is in Governor's Harbour, halfway down the coast, a town now dominated by a very active 53-acre **Club Med.** This club's specialty is scuba diving, with daily expeditions (including one to the Exuma Wall) for experienced divers, and a series of four lessons, leading to club certification, for beginners. There's also a complete photo lab for developing underwater pictures.

Other activities and special features include eight tennis courts, yoga, snorkeling, sailing, water-skiing, mini-clubs (for parents who want to bring their kids, but not see them during the day), and a circus workshop in which guests of all ages can learn Big Top skills from juggling to the trapeze.

In the Club Med tradition, one-week vacations ($920 plus airfare) include three meals a day, wine with lunch and dinner, and all activities. Telephone (800) 528–3100.

Another airport, in Rock Sound, serves the southern end of Eleuthera. The **Winding Bay Beach Resort** is just seven miles away. Although it closed its doors last season, Winding Bay has reopened under new management (Savoy Resorts), a new everything-included-in-the-room-rate system, and the old millionaire's estate atmosphere. There are a private beach, pool, tennis, water sports, entertainment, and 36 oceanview cottages, each with its own private patio. The double-room rates start at $255 per room, per night and include three meals, bar drinks, beer, wine at meals, sports, activities program, taxes, tips, and transportation to and from the airport. There is a two-night minimum stay. Rates vary, depending on season, length of stay, and the exact accommodations you ask for. Box 93, Rock Sound, Eleuthera, Bahamas, (800) 223–1588 or (212) 661–4540.

The **Cotton Bay Resort,** with 77 recently refurbished air-conditioned rooms ($254 MAP) and an 18-hole golf course, has an equally elegant atmosphere and a similar clientele. Tennis, water sports, a private beach, beautiful new landscaping, and pink cottages that open right onto the beach are among the attractions. Box 28, Rock Sound, Eleuthera, Bahamas. (809) 334–2101.

And then there is the **Windermere Island Club,** 18 miles from the Rock Sound airport. Set on a private island, Windermere has been described as understated, luxurious, and just a trifle snobbish. If you can get a reservation, you'll find 22 air-conditioned villas, rooms and apartments ($300–$1,000 AP), a private beach, pool, water sports, six tennis courts, and international cuisine. Like all the Rock Sound resorts, this one tends to be more formal during the winter season. Box 25, Rock Sound, Eleuthera, Bahamas. (809) 332–2538.

Eleuthera has never officially been named the Bahamas' most beautiful island, but there are many who would give it their vote. Lush green foliage, resorts practically draped in bougainvillea, and 17th-century architecture add up to a very visual travel experience. If possible, try to see some of its natural glories on your own.

A long taxi trip up and down this 110-mile-long island (but only five miles wide at its widest point) could blow the budget, but there are several local car rental companies in Palmetto Point (next to Governor's Harbour), Rock Sound, and Harbour Island itself.

Sights to go out of your way for include the Glass Window (a spot near Upper Bogue where the island becomes so narrow that you're driving with the Atlantic on one side of the road and the bay on the other) and the pineapple plantation in Gregory Town.

Bahamasair has daily flights to the three Eleuthera airports. There also are direct flights from Miami to all three.

The Abacos

Not every American was happy about the Declaration of Independence. A number were so upset that they left, sailing for The Abacos in the 1780s. Some English settlers were already there, and the descendants of both groups give this 130-mile-long island chain a true New England flavor. The Abacos may be one of the most tourist-developed Out Islands, but few have accused it of being spoiled by progress.

TREASURE CAY

The largest and most formal resort in the Abacos is the **Treasure Cay Beach Hotel & Villas.** You can arrive by boat, as many visitors do, or fly to Treasure Cay. A $10 taxi ride over a bumpy dirt road brings you to the hotel's front door.

There are luxuries here in the 122 hotel rooms, cottages, and villas that you won't find in other Out Island hotels. Even the standard rooms ($118–$140) in the main building are large, with two double beds, sand-colored carpet, and a garden view, plus satellite TV and a dressing room with open closet. There are no tele-phones (you can wait your turn for the one in the lobby) and the bathroom provides the world's smallest towels.

The fir-and-stucco duplex Harbour House accom-modations are the resort's finest. You can rent a single bedroom, a one-bedroom suite, or various combinations thereof. The suite includes a small kitchen, a living room with sliding glass doors and marina view, and very pri-vate loft bedroom with adjoining bath. Rates for rooms and suites begin at $118.

If you prefer cottage-style comfort ($180–$310), you have a choice of two-bedroom ocean-view apartments, two-bedroom villas, or one-bedroom villas. The one bedrooms are the most attractive, with floral print sofas and open kitchens with bars.

The marina may be Treasure Cay's main attraction, but the secluded beach alone is worth the trip. Spectacu-lar at first sight, it has white sand so soft and fine it feels a little like powder between your toes. The light aqua water is as calm and clear as a pool.

Treasure Cay is one of those self-contained resorts you never have to leave. You have an 18-hole golf course, ten tennis courts, five swimming pools, sailing, snorkel-ing, scuba diving, water-skiing, bikes for rent, and fishing boats for charter. The gift shop has all the china, crystal, and perfume you might have looked for in Nassau. The resort shopping center includes a liquor store, a beauty salon, a supermarket, and post office.

Meals are at the harbor-view Spinnaker Restaurant or the slightly more formal Abaco Room. This is one of the few Out Islands resorts where men wear jackets for dinner.

The Treasure Cay crowd is as polished as the resort: men with well-kept beards and good haircuts, women with salon-highlighted hair and perfectly even tans. This is the kind of place you might hear a 20ish blonde insist-ing on immediate checkout because she's made up with her husband of three weeks—and her parents' plane is waiting to whisk her back to him.

Treasure Cay Services, 2801 Ponce de Leon Blvd.,

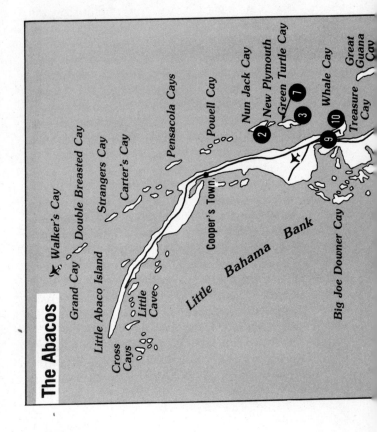

Points of Interest

1) Abaco Inn
2) Albert Lowe Museum
3) Bluff House
4) Conch Inn

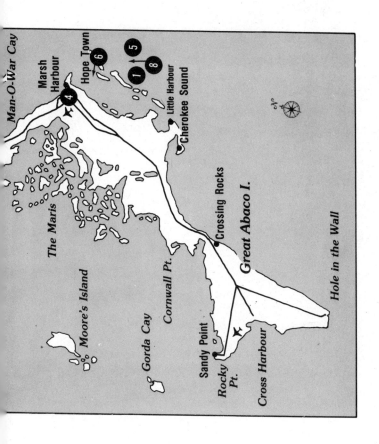

5) Elbow Cay Beach Club
6) Great Abaco Beach Hotel
7) Green Turtle Club
8) Hope Town Harbour Lodge
9) Treasure Cay Beach Hotel & Villas
10) Treasure Cay Marina

Coral Gables, FL 33134, (305) 444–8381 or (800) 327–1584.

GREEN TURTLE CAY

For a more casual mood, stay at the **Green Turtle Club** on nearby Green Turtle Cay. Taxi ($10) from airport to ferry ($4) and zip over to the hotel dock where debonair British manager Martin Havill often meets the boat personally.

Your first glimpse will be the green canopy and some very relaxed people having drinks on the porch of the Tipsy Turtle Bar. The bar's decor reflects the club mood —"barefoot British," with burgees hanging from the ceiling and dollar bills plastered along the wall, all autographed by former guests, from Jimmy Carter to Christopher Reeve.

Walk past the 50-foot saltwater pool with its green striped cushion lounges. Your Abaco pine cottage has carpeting, air-conditioning, and sliding glass doors ($86 –$110 double, summer). The beach is a short walk away. If you're arriving in your own boat, you might radio ahead to reserve one of the Seaside Villas ($100–$250) instead—possibly the only "hotel rooms" in the Bahamas that let you tie up at your very own dock.

Activities include boat rentals, snorkeling, windsurfing, bonefishing, and deep-sea fishing. No tennis or golf, but nobody seems to mind. The two biggest weeks of the year are the June fishing tournament and the July regatta.

Green Turtle Club, Green Turtle Cay, Abaco, Bahamas. (305) 842–3109 or (809) 367–2572.

And then there is **Bluff House,** an elegant hideaway on Green Turtle Cay. When you arrive by boat, there's a short uphill hike through tall trees to the main building. The handsome lounge has wicker chairs with floral cushions and a louvered glass wall looking out onto the 40-foot-pool. The dining room has ceramic tile floors, beamed ceilings, and a sea view.

People come to Bluff House for the seclusion and natural beauty. Rates range from $90 (standard room) to $218 (four people in a two-bedroom villa with kitchen). Suites ($106) are the most popular of the resort's 36 rooms. That means a bedroom with pickled-pine paneling, a pine staircase leading down to the living room, and a kitchenette and patio-on-the-sea.

Tennis, boat rentals, sailing, bonefishing, deep-sea fishing, and windsurfing are among the activities to choose from. Your hosts are American owners Melissa and Leslie Davies.

Bluff House, Green Turtle Cay, Abaco, Bahamas. (305) 941–6987. No credit cards.

New Plymouth

Wherever you stay, you must visit the village of New Plymouth. The ferry takes you there. New Plymouth is an excellent place to meet people; the list of sights is so well-established that you'll keep running into the same people all day.

There are two must-sees in town. One, right at the end of the ferry dock, is the **Albert Lowe Museum.** At first glance, the $3 admission may seem high. But this small house behind the white picket fence is chock-full of Abaco history. Local artist Alton Lowe named it for his father, whose paintings of local subjects are inside. You'll also find six rooms filled with photos and artifacts designed to help preserve the island's culture.

And you cannot leave without visiting **Miss Emily's Blue Bee Bar.** Just turn left as you enter town, make a left at the cemetery, and you're there. Miss Emily's looks rundown, compared to the pink, mustard-yellow, and pistachio-green houses nearby, but a lot of famous people have been here and left their photos and business cards to paper the walls. Have a Goombay Smash and hope to meet someone sexy from the yacht next door.

MARSH HARBOUR

The Abacos' other center of tourism is in Marsh Harbour. Fly or take a boat; getting there overland from Treasure Cay is a 20-mile trek over incredibly bumpy roads. Taxi drivers charge $70 or more round-trip, and deserve every cent.

The Conch Inn has been the boaters' social center here for years. In The Conch Crawl, where you can have breakfast, drinks, or lunch, there are bulletin-board messages, mail for the regulars, and ship-to-shore radio calls constantly coming in. In late afternoon, make new friends poolside by watching or joining in the daily Wallyball game (named for former owner Wally Smith, but also a play on words—Bahamians pronounce their V's as W's).

The Conch Inn restaurant, in a separate building, is *the* place for dinner. Its Conch Out Bar is an attractive living-room setting, all white with hot pink and yellow accents. The restaurant itself has a combination of wicker chairs and director's chairs at white tables, and bamboo shades rolled high so diners can gaze into the harbor. Specialties include the seafood plate (conch, shrimp, and grouper) and turtle steak.

The inn's decor is nothing to write home about, but each room is air-conditioned and clean. Year-round rates are $75 double. Conch Inn Resort, Box 434, Marsh Harbour, Abaco, Bahamas. (809) 367–2800.

The **Great Abaco Beach Hotel** is a much more elegant Marsh Harbour address. At first, you'll see only a long dirt road, but then the grand green lawn appears, dotted with towering palm trees bent by the winds. The pool and white sand beach are just beyond.

The rooms at Great Abaco ($85 double) are luxurious by Out Island standards. They're spacious, with air-conditioning, carpeting, two double beds with bamboo headboards, print draperies, and a bath with a separate dressing area. Every room has a beach-view balcony.

Each villa ($150) has a living room, bedroom, open kitchen, and Abaco pine deck.

Night life? On the nights they have live music at the Dolphin Bar, you'll find a lively, youngish crowd of tourists and locals dancing the early morning hours away. If you meet someone nice there, have a candlelight dinner the next evening in the large lobby-level dining room. Red banquettes, hanging plants, and a pine cathedral ceiling are the setting for dishes like lobster, turtle steak, and a special Caesar salad for two.

Activities include tennis, snorkeling, diving, fishing trips, bike rentals, and sailboat charters (with or without crew).

Great Abaco Beach Hotel, Box 419, Marsh Harbour, Abaco, Bahamas. (809) 367–2158.

HOPE TOWN

A more secluded area near Marsh Harbour is Hopetown on Elbow Cay (ferry, $6) where there are three hotels to choose from.

Hope Town Harbour Lodge looks as though it belongs in a New England seaside resort. This white clapboard house with pink trim has 19 carpeted hotel rooms ($70–$90) and one entire house ($625 per week). If you need air-conditioning, ask for one of the downstairs rooms (#1–5, 9, and 14).

The dining-room menu changes every night. Your choices will be Continental, perhaps grouper Dijonnaise or veal piccata. The Pool Bar is the site of the hotel's locally famous Sunday Champagne Brunch. If you're staying here, you automatically get reservations to this huge $15 buffet. Otherwise, write or radio a week or two ahead of time. The ferry lets you off at the hotel's front door.

Hope Town Harbour Lodge, Hope Town, Abaco, Bahamas. Telephone (809) 367–2277 or (800) 626–5690.

The Abaco Inn is one of those places that wouldn't

impress you if you saw it vacant, but it draws the right people to its splendid isolation and overcomes the landscape. There are only ten cottages, so reserve ahead for what you want. All the oceanfront cottages ($105) have king-size beds, bookshelves, walk-in open closets, baths with a shower only, beamed ceilings, and ceiling fans. If you want lovers' privacy, ask for #5; it faces the ocean directly, and you can relax in your own hammock, hidden by foliage. The harbour rooms ($95) offer the same features, plus sliding glass doors and air-conditioning. The best two, #9 and #7, face the bay directly.

You might spend your days at the saltwater pool, perched dramatically on a cliff, and your evenings by the piano or fireplace in the pine-paneled lobby/lounge.

The inn offers diving, snorkeling, sailing trips, and all the usual activities, but meals are the big event. Where you eat literally depends on which way the wind is blowing; tables are set for comfort, as well as view. And even if you aren't staying here, you can sail in for the $18 fixed-price dinner. One recent menu offered a choice of roast duck, veal piccata, and coquille St. Jacques, plus some unusual dishes like peanut butter soup and zucchini bread.

Your only problem could be getting there. The normal $12 ferry takes you to Hope Town Harbour Lodge. To get to the Abaco Inn, you either ask the captain to radio ahead so the inn van will meet you there, or charter a boat ($30) to take you directly to the Abaco Inn dock.

Abaco Inn, Hope Town, Elbow Cay, Abaco, Bahamas. (809) 367–2666.

The Elbow Cay Beach Inn, run by a charming Danish couple, has become the center of Elbow Cay's night life, thanks to the live music (Wednesday to Saturday nights) and the smorgasbord. Other assets include a freshwater pool and a 38-foot boat, so guests can go diving or snorkeling.

The 82-acre resort has 30 rooms ($74–$94) and, although the decor (thatched ceilings and cement bed bases in some) may not suit every taste, some of the views are spectacular. Five rooms allow you to lie in bed and look out sliding glass doors directly onto the water.

Elbow Cay Beach Inn, Hope Town, Abaco, Bahamas. Telephone (809) 367–2748.

MAN O' WAR CAY

The day trip not to miss is the one to Man O' War Cay, the boat-building capital of the Bahamas. Take the same ferry that brought you to Elbow Cay (owned by the Alburys, as is most of Man O' War) and plan to spend half a day or so. Be prepared: There are no real restaurants here and no liquor is sold.

The roads here are just wide sidewalks (no cars), and the road to the beach is lined with shrubbery and trees.

Dock & Dine is the first building you'll see, with take-out food on one side and a dive shop on the other. They rent and sell equipment and organize dive trips. Turn left to see several examples of old-fashioned boat building. You'll also pass several gift shops, offering books about the area, T-shirts, and the like. The Seaside Boutique has a good selection of Androsia, some from Andros and some made here from their own designs. The Sail Shop is the one stop everyone wants to make. You can watch local women sew canvas items, then buy your favorite—bags, hats, carry-alls, or shaving kits (most under $30). Finally, for great ice cream, visit the Bite Site.

If you're interested in a get-away-from-it-all vacation, there are 20 or so two-bedroom cottages for rent at about $350 per week, including utilities, linens, and kitchenware. Some are on or near the beach. For information, call the Man O' War marina, (809) 367–2306.

Getting to the Abacos: There are direct Bahamasair flights from Miami to Treasure Cay. Scheduled charters also fly from Florida to Treasure Cay and Marsh Harbour. Bahamasair has daily flights from both Nassau and Miami to Marsh Harbour.

The Exumas

Fly to the Exumas, if only for the view. Even scenery-
weary pilots still marvel at the surrealistic blue, green,
and white patterns of the Exuma Cays as they are seen
from the air. The shimmers, ridges, and gradations of
color where islands seem to float in the air and the sea
seems to blend with the sky are worth fighting for a
window seat to watch (right side of the plane on your way
to George Town; left side coming back).

Of course, the Exuma Cays mean challenge and
beauty to boaters, too; this is the yachting capital of the
Bahamas. In the Exumas, the bonefishing is remarkable.
The snorkeling at the Exuma Land and Sea Park is
breathtaking. And if there are two of you, you can rent
a boat and find a private cay all your own.

A taxi from the George Town airport will cost $8.75
per couple. Renting a car (about $200 per week, unlimit-
ed mileage) or boat is a must if you're planning to see the
sights.

The first thing you'll learn is that George Town isn't
a town at all, but just a scattering of buildings with no
central district. If there is one landmark, it's the **Peace &
Plenty Hotel,** a pink and white inn that began life as a

90

sponge warehouse and was strictly a yacht club until a few decades ago.

Today, it's the center of social life for yachtsmen and landlubbers alike. The cozy bar, with its blue plank banquettes, its collection of burgees, and the wooden name plates of ships like *Fascinatin' Bitch* and *Sun Sign,* is the sort of place where everybody calls the bartenders by name. And on the nights that the hotel features live music, the bar and pool deck are as raucous as a fraternity party—but with guests of all ages, races, and creeds.

Peace & Plenty's rooms are clean and pleasant and, by the time you read this, completely refurbished. A typical guest room has a tile floor, double bed, beige rattan furniture, marble vanity and shower, air-conditioning, and a good-sized balcony. This is one of the few hotels in all of the Bahamas that bothers to leave shampoo, shower cap, and scented English soap in the bath for each new guest.

There are eight waterfront rooms (#5, 6, 9, 10, 15, 16, 20, and 21) at $96 per day. But for $6 less per day, rooms #17, 18, and 19 give you almost as good a sea view. Three poolside rooms (#1, 2, and 3) have been turned into garden suites, with sitting rooms whose sliding glass doors will open right onto the pool area.

The pool here is small, as are all Exuma hotel pools. What you'll want to do is take the ferry (free to hotel guests) over to Stocking Island, where a stretch of white sand beach that's perfect for sunning and swimming awaits you. Pick the right morning or the right cove, and it could be just you and a long-legged sea bird among the pines and sand dunes. The "beach club" here is a one-room wooden shelter, serving sandwiches and drinks. This is the perfect island for that romantic picnic for two.

Meals in the Peace & Plenty are as casual as the restaurant's blue and white lawn furniture decor—until evening. Then it's a formal five-course dinner (approximate tab $20) that, oddly enough, you order by writing out your own dinner check.

Peace & Plenty Hotel, Box 55, George Town, Exuma, Bahamas. (305) 462–2551 or (809) 336–2551.

George Town's small choice of shops are right across the street. **Sandpiper** has an excellent selection of

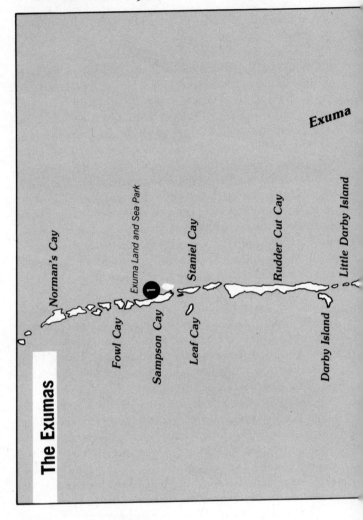

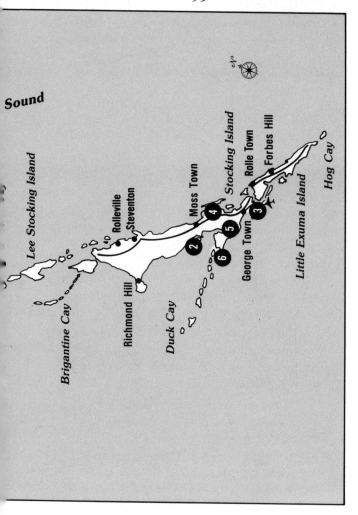

Points of Interest

1) Exuma Land & Sea Park
2) Out Island Inn
3) Peace & Plenty Hotel
4) Regatta Point Apartments
5) Sandpiper
6) Two Turtles Inn

paperbacks, from Hemingway to Harold Robbins, plus books about the Bahamas, resortwear, and silk screens done by the owner. The **Peace & Plenty Boutique** has a large selection of Androsia batik resort wear.

The **Pieces of 8 Hotel** is a motel-like building set on a hill, so that every room has a sea view. The 33 rooms ($60, single or double) have balconies, carpet, air-conditioning, and sliding-door closets. The glass-walled restaurant, overlooking the pool, serves all three meals. Lunch entrées are $3.50–$5.50; dinner is $7.75–$15.50. A dive operation is run in the building across the street.

The **Out Island Inn,** just down the road, is its sister operation—and by far the more glamorous of the two. You'll enter via a curving tree-lined driveway and probably spot the pool and tennis courts before being taken to your room.

Each of the 88 air-conditioned rooms ($200–$210 AP) has two double beds, a carpet, balcony, and bath with marble vanity, plus a dressing table with the mirror and the plugs in the right places. Louvered floor-to-ceiling windows give the exteriors an almost Japanese look, and greenery growing on the stone walls add an unusual ivy-covered campus touch.

The Reef Bar is the inn's huge seaside restaurant, set on its own peninsula. You'll find typically nautical decor, casual food at lunch ($3–$6), more ambitious dishes like beef medallions topped with crabmeat and Monterey Jack cheese at dinner ($10.50–$16.50), and a lot of action on the nights they have live music. There's a stone pier right outside where you can fish—or just watch the seagulls taking a break.

Back in "town," you'll find the **Two Turtles Inn.** Valerie Noyes, the charming British woman who welcomed guests from Prince Philip to King Constantine of Greece during her years at Peace & Plenty, became manager a few years ago and promptly began to transform a somewhat run-down property into a European-style inn. By the time you read this, it will be the only hotel in the Exumas to offer satellite TV.

The 14 rooms ($60) all have one double bed and one twin, plus carpeting, a bath with shower, and ceiling fans. Only rooms #10, 11, 12, 14, and 15 are air-conditioned. Reserve ahead to get one of the four efficiencies (same price) with kitchenettes behind louvered doors.

Meals (burgers to lobster, $4–$12) are served inside the half-timbered dining room or in the shady central courtyard.

Two Turtles Inn, Box 51, George Town, Exuma, Bahamas. (809) 336–2545.

The **Regatta Point Apartments,** just past the government dock road, is a lovely place to stay, particularly if you're planning to do your own cooking. The palm-lined driveway leads you to the five-room building. The two rooms downstairs are large efficiencies (about 23' × 15'), with open kitchen, louvered closets, and bathrooms with back doors (the better to track water and sand into, rather than into the main room). Each suite has high ceilings, tile floors, a full kitchen behind louvered doors, a separate bedroom, a bath with a large vanity, and a back door to patio. All rooms are $76 double; the early birds get the suites.

Despite the name and location, this is not where the revelers stay at Regatta time. Expect a quieter, almost pastoral mood with a tiny beach and a spectacular sea view.

Regatta Point Apartments, Box 6, George Town, Exuma. (809) 336–2206.

The place to go for authentic Bahamian food is **Eddie's Edgewater Club.** Just turn left at "the pond" (Victoria Lake) and keep going until you see a green building, usually with lots of local men hanging around outside. This is a family place (Victor and Andrea Brown run it; the original Eddie is Andrea's father), but it can look rough, so women probably won't feel comfortable alone here. Dinner prices range from $5 for chicken livers to $13.50 for lobster. Other popular dishes include turtle steak and red snapper. The very Bahamian weekend special is chicken, sheep tongue, or turtle souse ($3.50). No credit cards.

There is one major new hotel making news in the Exumas. **The Flamingo Bay Hotel and Villas** opened some of its doors last season, and construction may be completed by the time of your 1988 visit. Near the airport and just outside George Town, Flamingo Bay could very well turn out to be the island's most luxurious accommodations by far. On the drawing board are 37 air-conditioned two-bedroom suites with swimming pool, sauna, and maid service, nine two- and three-bedroom Palmetto Court suites with the same amenities, and a total of 150 villas.

It's hard to predict the crowd you'll find here in seasons to come. Because accommodations will range from one- to five-bedroom layouts, it is likely to be a favorite of honeymooners, large families, as well as all the groups in between. On the other hand, one British travel writer has already described the place as a "new Garden of Eden," and has predicted that the rich and famous soon will be enjoying their lifestyles here.

The developers—Elizabeth Harbour, Exuma Ltd.—are talking about tennis courts, private beaches, and health clubs, at least for the top-of-the-line accommodations. Satellite TV and direct dialing to the U.S. were among the first services installed. Flamingo Bay is a time-share resort. Like many other properties of its kind, however, it offers standard hotel rental arrangements as well.

Just 13 rooms had opened at press time. First-season rates were $155–$230 for double rooms, $110–$135 for one-bedroom villas, and $155–$235 for the two-bedrooms villas.

Flamingo Bay Hotel & Villas, Box 90, George Town, Exuma. (809) 336–2661.

Unhappily, it may be only a matter of time until the Exumas are discovered by vacationers other than the ever-loyal yachting set. (George Town is on Great Exuma, but that island is only one in a 150-mile-long chain). The Exumas are made up of more than 300 islands, many of them small and uninhabited, running from just 40 miles southeast of Nassau to the Tropic of Cancer itself.) But, fortunately for those who hold the Exumas close to their hearts, this destination has a long way to go before it risks losing its rustic Out Island charm.

When you feel like sightseeing, drive to the north of Great Exuma toward Rolleville, preferably with a guide who can identify the old plantations and other historical sights along the way. Stop at **Fisherman's Inn,** the restaurant that everybody is talking about.

There are scheduled charter flights to George Town from Fort Lauderdale, Miami and Eleuthera (North Eleuthera and Rock Sound). Bahamasair flies here from Nassau.

Andros

You won't have to tell the taxi driver where you're going.
If you are American and getting off a plane in Andros
Town, he'll approach and ask, "**Small Hope Bay
Lodge**?," and he'll be right. Although Andros is the larg-
est of the Bahamian islands, it is also one of the least
explored. Small Hope is one of its few real resorts.

Most of the guests at Small Hope are avid or avidly
aspiring scuba divers. The world's third largest barrier
reef is here, and the underwater beauty is dazzling
enough at 10 or 15 feet to convince novices to don tank
and regulator for a shallow dive.

Others swear they'd come here for the dinner conversation alone. North American owners Dick and Rosi
Birch are gradually passing the torch to a new generation
—his kids, hers, and theirs, now grown, very ably running
the show and continuing to set a special tone.

If you've never been to one of these 20-cottage resorts with honor bars and first-name informality, relax.
You'll like it.

Imagine this typical day: You wake up early, an
ocean breeze rustling through your Androsia batik curtains. You could compare your cottage to a hotel room

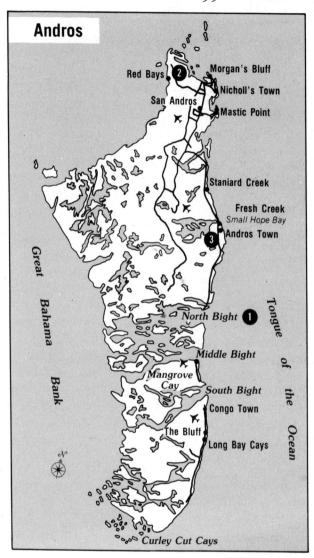

Points of Interest

1) Great Barrier Reef
2) Red Bay Village
3) Small Hope Bay Lodge

and find it a bit too rustic. But you've already mellowed out (which happens within 24 hours here). So you see it instead as the camp cabin of your childhood, redecorated for adult life with carpeting, big thick towels, Androsia pillowcases, and wall hangings. Some cabins even have water beds.

You dress in a swimsuit and cover-up or T-shirt, then stroll to the main building for breakfast. The dining/gathering room has a beamed ceiling, louvered windows on all sides, and a stone fireplace. There are six tables, most for six people each, and pine-plank chairs. Help yourself to juice, coffee, cereal, and toast, then order eggs or waffles from the kitchen.

The morning dive boat leaves from the pier at 9:30, heading for a deep dive and a shallow one. If you're not a diver, you now have the resort all to yourself. The others will be back just in time for lunch.

There are a few spare moments, however, for a pre-lunch drink. Pour yourself a beer or glass of wine or mix yourself a drink at the bar, take the card that has your name on it out of the slot, write in what you've had, and carry your glass out to a lawn chair in the shade.

Lunch is indoors, buffet-style. And as soon as you've finished, it's time to think about the afternoon dive. Or skip the dive that day to lie on the beach, wind down in the hot tub, or schedule a Swedish massage.

The others will be back in time to slowly "dress" for dinner. When you wash out your wet swimsuits and T-shirts, there are pegs outside your door to hang them on for fresh air drying. On a dark night, this also helps you identify your cabin on the way home.

Conch fritters are served at cocktail hour. But get there early; they go fast. Dinner is usually a choice of meat or seafood entrée, preceded by a buffet of appetizers. Afterward, guests chat or start a game of Trivial Pursuit.

Feel like a nightcap? Pour yourself a Courvoisier, sign for it, and stroll home in the moonlight. This can't be camp. When did the counselor ever let you bring brandy back to the room or offer nightly turndown service?

The resort also offers all-day trips that go out at 9:30

A.M. and return at 4:30 P.M. or so. Each trip includes a morning dive, afternoon dive, and a packed lunch served on an island where guests also can swim, lie on the beach, or snorkel.

Warning: Don't bring fancy clothes to Small Hope Bay. Dressing for dinner generally means taking a shower. Rosi Birch herself is likely to turn up barefoot in one of her long Androsia batik dresses (she's founder and owner of Androsia). High-heeled sandals for women seem like formalwear here. Anyway, your cabin's front lawn is the beach, and you'll just get sand in your shoes if you wear them.

If you must look for imperfections, here: The beach and the swimming from shore aren't much. But swimming from the dive boat in clear, cool water on perfect sky-blue days makes up for it. The daytime landscape is far from lush. But the night sky is so clear that many visitors spot stars they've never seen before. A frog might turn up in your bathroom, but he'll leave peacefully. There's a barracuda living under the dock, but his name is George and everybody likes him.

Small Hope is "a world of its own," but guests are secluded from the outside world, not from each other. And when someone feels a need for more action, they head for Samson's, the local disco, to watch the break dancers.

Summer isn't off-season for the divers who come here. You won't find many singles (check the names and room numbers on the honor-bar slots to see who's alone) but you're unlikely to be lonely if you come alone. The couples and families from all across the U.S. are a relatively sophisticated but friendly bunch.

Summer rates ($190 double) include all three meals and use of sailboat, windsurfing equipment, bicycles, and hot tub. Daytime dives are $25; night dives, $30.

You can fly here from Nassau by Bahamasair. There are also charters, including Small Hope's own plane, directly from Fort Lauderdale. Taxi from the airport is $12 per couple, plus $1.50 per additional passenger.

Small Hope Bay Lodge, Box N-1131, Fresh Creek, Andros. (800) 223–6961, (305) 463–9130, or (809) 368–2014.

If you have a chance to explore the dense forests of Andros, keep your eyes open for Chickcharnies. They're the legendary red-eyed elves who hang by their tails from trees, can turn their heads 360 degrees on their shoulders, and create all kinds of mischief.

Bimini

Bimini breaks all the rules for what a Bahamian island is supposed to be. In a way, little has changed here since Ernest Hemingway spent much of the 1930s on or near Bimini's waters—waters that inspired him to write *The Old Man and The Sea* and to set his *Islands in the Stream* novella here. This is still the big-game fishing capital of the world. The average visitor is a Florida fisherman who stays just 1.7 days.

Bimini is our closest neighbor, just 50 miles off the Florida coast—thus its nickname, "Gateway to the Bahamas." And it is certainly the most Americanized of the islands.

Current American rock hits blare from storefronts along North Bimini's main street. And you may find the barmaid at the Red Lion Pub standing under a Miami Dolphins poster as she watches the CBS afternoon soaps. One hotelier claims he's never seen a single dollar of Bahamian currency cross his front desk.

Summer is high season in Bimini. The time to go for blue or white marlin is April through July; for broadbill swordfish, June through September; and for snapper, April through September. But this is a year-round desti-

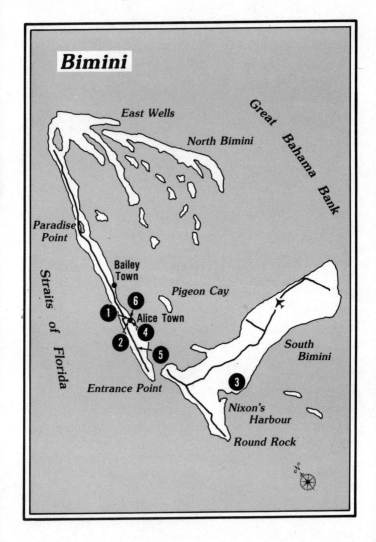

Points of Interest

1) The Anchorage
2) Bimini Big Game Fishing Club
3) Cavelle Pond (Fountain of Youth)
4) The Compleat Angler
5) Queen's Highway
6) Red Lion Pub

nation. Bonefishing is good throughout the year, and both wahoo and grouper, not to mention snapper, barracuda, dolphin, and shark, are at their most catchable in the winter.

The **Bimini Big Game Fishing Club** is the place to stay. This haven of taste in what the brochures refer to as a "down-to-earth salty" ("rowdy" might be a more accurate word) town maintains a members-only atmosphere behind its black gates.

Whether you plan to spend your days battling with marlin or basking in the sun, you'll appreciate the hotel's 23-foot-long balconied rooms with carpet, air-conditioning, and modern furniture. All have two beds and are decorated with a "studio" feel—because so much entertaining (read: partying) goes on in the rooms themselves.

The club's cottages are even nicer, with kitchenettes (sink and fridge only) and louvered-door closets. The resort's three suites, the most glamorous lodgings of all, each have a modern living room, kitchenette, bedroom with terrace, bath, and separate dressing room. All rooms have cable TV.

Most guests are out in their boats at midday, and BBGFC will prepare box lunches for them. But if you're staying behind to enjoy the tennis court or the pool with its brick deck, light lunches are available—sandwiches, salads, and a choice of hot dishes.

Dinner, however, is the event. Entrée prices at the pool-view dining room start at $12.95 (cracked conch) and go up to $22 (grilled lobster tails). Baby Como salmon is even flown in from Washington state.

You don't have to be rich to stay here, but many guests are. Chartering the resort's 41-foot *Sir Tones II* will cost $600 per day. At least one package vacation here, however, includes a complimentary day's rental of a 16-foot center console outboard boat.

Rooms are $96, cottages $116, and penthouses $215, double or single. Marina dockage is $.60 per foot per day; small craft up to 30 feet long are $18 per day. 2857 S.W. 27th Ave., Miami, FL 33133. (800) 327–4149, (809) 347–2391, or (305) 444–7480.

Most guests arrive in their own boats or by ferry. Some come by seaplane.

Let's get our geography straight. "The Biminis" are two islands—north and south. Besides the airport, the only thing to see in South Bimini is a pond believed to be the Fountain of Youth that Ponce De Leon tried to find. North Bimini is the place you'll visit, and Alice Town is its one-street "capital."

Flying here from Miami/Fort Lauderdale or Paradise Island via Chalk's seaplane can be an interesting experience. The aircraft interior is cramped, but takeoffs and landings—with sea spray covering your window—are exciting. Unless your luggage is heavy, you can walk anywhere you want to go from here. The local taxi is a van that charges $3, no matter how long or short your trip.

The first important spot you'll encounter is the **Hi*-Star Disco** on your right. This stone building looks quiet enough by day, but it's the center of action at night until 3 A.M.

Bimini is not made for shopping sprees, but several small stores line the street, including a branch of the **Perfume Bar.**

The Compleat Angler, a dark green and white house on the left, is your first glimpse of the Bimini that Hemingway knew. Sadly, the hotel has seen fit to paint the words, "Home of Papa Ernest Hemingway" in huge letters on the building front.

Still, a place where the office and the bar are the same room can't be all bad. This bar is air-conditioned, its dark wood walls covered with an odd assortment of objects that range from straw hats to a fake shark's head. The wood is from kegs used during Bimini's rum-running heyday. This is the sort of place you'll feel really effete ordering a glass of white wine.

But it's the front room, with its fireplace and backgammon boards, that holds photos of Hemingway and friends landing the big ones almost half a century ago.

Incidentally, the Ponce de Leon bar in *Islands in the Stream* was patterned after this very place.

The Compleat Angler still qualifies as charming, but it could go over the edge at any moment. The 15 air-conditioned guest rooms won't win any prizes for luxury, but the price is right: $50 single, $60 double, and $70 deluxe. You can even rent Hemingway's old room. (#1).

Compleat Angler Hotel, Box 601, Alice Town, Bimini. (809) 347–2122.

The Anchorage is an attractive hillside house a little further on, all fresh white paint and blue trim, and an excellent lunch or dinner spot. The dining room has a spectacular view of blue-green sea, and entrées ($8.50–$17) range from omelettes to steak or lobster. Or order a $6.50 box lunch. The marina can charter you a 28-foot boat with captain and mate.

Bimini's Blue Water Ltd., Box 627, Bimini, Bahamas. (809) 347–2166.

The **Red Lion Pub** is on your right, just a bit up the road. This is an authentically down-home place with faded wallpaper and old red diner booths. The air-conditioned bayfront dining room is a good spot for a casual lunch or dinner (served from 6 P.M. on, Tuesdays through Sundays). Entrées range from $9 for chopped sirloin to $15.50 for lobster tails, steak, or shrimp.

Bimini is one of the most casual of all the Bahamian islands. Men shouldn't bother bringing jackets, much less ties. A dress code for dinner usually means that shoes are absolutely mandatory.

If you're a non-fisherperson, there is excellent scuba diving here. The most famous sight is a submerged stone wall off North Bimini, believed by some to be part of the lost continent of Atlantis.

More Family Islands

Everyone who writes about the Bahamas likes to mention that there are 700 islands. Of course, some are barely large enough to pitch a tent on, but a number have special sights, sounds, and experiences to offer. Even more undiscovered than the islands we've reported on so far, these range from a naturalist's preserve to the spot where Columbus discovered the New World (although the exact location has been called into question recently). When you're truly ready to leave civilization behind for a week or two, one of them could be the unspoiled vacation paradise you've been hoping to find.

ACKLINS ISLAND/ CROOKED ISLAND

Dotted with old lighthouses and separated only by a narrow passage (which you can cross by ferry), these two islands in the southern Bahamas can be considered one destination. Completely away from the Bahamas tourist circuit, this may well be the most peaceful vacation spot you've ever found.

The largest resort (16 rooms) is **Pittstown Point Landings Inn** at Crooked Island's northern tip. There you'll find diving, snorkeling, and boating. Double rooms are $75–$89.

Pittstown Point Landings Inn, c/o Bahamas Caribbean International, Box 9831, Mobile, AL 36691. (205) 666–4482 or (800) 336–2507.

There are Bahamasair flights between Nassau and the Colonel Hill Airport on Crooked Island.

THE BERRY ISLANDS

Lying right between Bimini and Nassau, the Berry Islands get their share of visitors—primarily divers, boaters, and fishermen who know by word of mouth what the area has to offer. The 12-square-mile island's one resort, a superb one, is the **Chub Cay Club,** located on the chain's southernmost cay. You'll find 55 rooms and villas, a complete scuba diving program, two tennis courts, and a 75-slip marina. Double rooms are $75–$125.

Chub Cay Club, Box 661067, Miami Springs, FL 33166. (809) 32–51490 or (305) 445–7830.

There are three Lucayan Air flights per week between Nassau and Chub Cay.

CAT ISLAND

At 200 feet above sea level, Cat Island doesn't even look like the Bahamas. It has towering cliffs, thick forests, the ruins of colonial plantations, and five moderately priced —but very small—resorts.

Greenwood Inn ($100 MAP) at Port Howe is the giant, with 16 rooms. You'll find boating, snorkeling, fishing, bicycling, a pool, the beach, and even a disco here. You're six miles from Cutlass Bay, the island's southernmost settlement.

Greenwood Inn, Port Howe, Cat Island, Bahamas; write or cable for reservations.

Other resorts are the ten-room **Hawk's Nest Club** at Devil's Point (tennis, diving, fishing, and beach); **Fernandez Bay Village,** with its eight housekeeping units near the airport; the **Cutlass Bay Yacht Club,** (eight rooms, tennis, boating, fishing, diving, pool, and beach); and the 12-room **Bridge Inn** in New Bight.

There are two Bahamasair flights per week between Nassau and Arthur's Town (at Cat Island's northern tip).

INAGUA

This, the most southerly of the Bahama islands, comes very close to being a naturalist's heaven. Here, at Lake Windsor, you'll find the largest colony (20,000+) of West Indian flamingoes in the world. Inagua's 234-square-mile wildlife reserve, which you can circuit by jeep tours, also has rare parrots, tree ducks, pelicans, blue heron, boar, and roseate spoonbills.

There are two guest houses, with a total of 13 rooms, in Matthew Town. **Ford's Inagua Inn** (telephone 277), just a mile from the airport, has five rooms, its own marina, and a nearby beach. Double rooms are $30. **Main House** (telephone 267), half a mile away, has eight rooms, air-conditioning, and a dining room. Double rooms are $40. The address for either is simply Matthew Town, Inagua, Bahamas.

The only trouble is, you can't take a day trip here—unless you have your own boat or plane. Bahamasair has two flights per week between Nassau and Matthew Town; if you come on Saturday, you have to stay until Tuesday.

LONG ISLAND

It lies just south of Exuma, attracting many of that island's yachtsmen to its varied landscape. Divers and fishermen come, too, to enjoy their sports and to sightsee among the churches, caves, and old plantations. Nature-lovers will want to visit Conception Island, just off Stella Maris, a sanctuary for both birds and green turtles.

The 42-room **Stella Maris Inn** ($80 double) is the resort of note, with fishing, boating, diving, snorkeling, water-skiing, tennis, a pool, and its own beach.

Stella Maris Inn, Stella Maris 30–105, Long Island, Bahamas. (809) 336–2106 or (809) 223–6510.

There are four Bahamasair flights per week between Nassau, Stella Maris, and Deadman's Cay (the airport farther south on Long Island).

RUM CAY

Just off Long Island's northeastern coast, Rum Cay (only 12 miles by seven) has a thriving dive resort. The 19-room **Rum Cay Club** specializes in scuba diving packages, but also offers catamarans, windsurfers, fishing, snorkeling, and lots of deserted beach. There's also a hot tub, game room, and—for serious underwater photographers—a photo lab.

Rum Cay Club, Box 22396, Fort Lauderdale, FL 33315. (305) 467–8355 or (809) 336–2142.

Some guests fly Bahamasair to Long Island or San

Salvador, then take private planes from there. Those who buy package vacations, however, take charter flights from Fort Lauderdale straight to Rum Cay.

SAN SALVADOR

This island is just as small as Rum Cay and virtually untouched, but you can hardly call it undiscovered. In fact, it was here that Christopher Columbus may have set foot on October 12, 1492. Today world-traveler fishermen, divers, and boaters consider it a find.

Its one resort, the highly respected **Riding Rock Inn,** (24 rooms and 10 villas) reopened under new management just a season or two ago. Double rooms are $80; cottages, $125. Riding Rock Inn, San Salvador. (809) 332–2631.

Bahamasair has two flights per week between Nassau and San Salvador.

Index

FODOR'S TRAVEL GUIDES

Here is a complete list of Fodor's Travel Guides, available in current editions; most are also available in a British edition published by Hodder & Stoughton.

U.S. GUIDES

Alaska
American Cities (Great Travel Values)
Arizona including the Grand Canyon
Atlantic City & the New Jersey Shore
Boston
California
Cape Cod & the Islands of Martha's Vineyard & Nantucket
Carolinas & the Georgia Coast
Chesapeake
Chicago
Colorado
Dallas/Fort Worth
Disney World & the Orlando Area (Fun in)
Far West
Florida
Forth Worth (see Dallas)
Galveston (see Houston)
Georgia (see Carolinas)
Grand Canyon (see Arizona)
Greater Miami & the Gold Coast
Hawaii
Hawaii (Great Travel Values)
Houston & Galveston
I-10: California to Florida
I-55: Chicago to New Orleans
I-75: Michigan to Florida
I-80: San Francisco to New York
I-95: Maine to Miami
Jamestown (see Williamsburg)
Las Vegas including Reno & Lake Tahoe (Fun in)
Los Angeles & Nearby Attractions
Martha's Vineyard (see Cape Cod)
Maui (Fun in)
Nantucket (see Cape Cod)
New England
New Jersey (see Atlantic City)
New Mexico
New Orleans
New Orleans (Fun in)
New York City
New York City (Fun in)
New York State
Orlando (see Disney World)
Pacific North Coast
Philadelphia
Reno (see Las Vegas)
Rockies
San Diego & Nearby Attractions
San Francisco (Fun in)
San Francisco plus Marin County & the Wine Country
The South
Texas
U.S.A.
Virgin Islands (U.S. & British)

Virginia
Waikiki (Fun in)
Washington, D.C.
Williamsburg, Jamestown & Yorktown

FOREIGN GUIDES

Acapulco (see Mexico City)
Acapulco (Fun in)
Amsterdam
Australia, New Zealand & the South Pacific
Austria
The Bahamas
The Bahamas (Fun in)
Barbados (Fun in)
Beijing, Guangzhou & Shanghai
Belgium & Luxembourg
Bermuda
Brazil
Britain (Great Travel Values)
Canada
Canada (Great Travel Values)
Canada's Maritime Provinces plus Newfoundland & Labrador
Cancún, Cozumel, Mérida & the Yucatán
Caribbean
Caribbean (Great Travel Values)
Central America
Copenhagen (see Stockholm)
Cozumel (see Cancún)
Eastern Europe
Egypt
Europe
Europe (Budget)
France
France (Great Travel Values)
Germany: East & West
Germany (Great Travel Values)
Great Britain
Greece
Guangzhou (see Beijing)
Helsinki (see Stockholm)
Holland
Hong Kong & Macau
Hungary
India, Nepal & Sri Lanka
Ireland
Israel
Italy
Italy (Great Travel Values)
Jamaica (Fun in)
Japan
Japan (Great Travel Values)
Jordan & the Holy Land
Kenya
Korea
Labrador (see Canada's Maritime Provinces)
Lisbon
Loire Valley
London

London (Fun in)
London (Great Travel Values)
Luxembourg (see Belgium)
Macau (see Hong Kong)
Madrid
Mazatlan (see Mexico's Baja)
Mexico
Mexico (Great Travel Values)
Mexico City & Acapulco
Mexico's Baja & Puerto Vallarta, Mazatlan, Manzanillo, Copper Canyon
Montreal (Fun in)
Munich
Nepal (see India)
New Zealand
Newfoundland (see Canada's Maritime Provinces)
1936 . . . on the Continent
North Africa
Oslo (see Stockholm)
Paris
Paris (Fun in)
People's Republic of China
Portugal
Province of Quebec
Puerto Vallarta (see Mexico's Baja)
Reykjavik (see Stockholm)
Rio (Fun in)
The Riviera (Fun on)
Rome
St. Martin/St. Maarten (Fun in)
Scandinavia
Scotland
Shanghai (see Beijing)
Singapore
South America
South Pacific
Southeast Asia
Soviet Union
Spain
Spain (Great Travel Values)
Sri Lanka (see India)
Stockholm, Copenhagen, Oslo, Helsinki & Reykjavik
Sweden
Switzerland
Sydney
Tokyo
Toronto
Turkey
Vienna
Yucatán (see Cancún)
Yugoslavia

SPECIAL-INTEREST GUIDES

Bed & Breakfast Guide: North America
Royalty Watching
Selected Hotels of Europe
Selected Resorts and Hotels of the U.S.
Ski Resorts of North America
Views to Dine by around the World

AVAILABLE AT YOUR LOCAL BOOKSTORE OR WRITE TO FODOR'S TRAVEL PUBLICATIONS, INC., 201 EAST 50th STREET, NEW YORK, NY 10022.